MILLCLOSE

The Mine That Drowned

MILLCLOSE

THE MINE THAT DROWNED

by
Lynn Willies, Keith Gregory and
Harry Parker

Scarthin Books, Cromford, Derbyshire
Peak District Mines Historical Society Ltd
1989

Opposite: 1. Frontispiece: Harold Wild of Winster, mine-deputy in the 1930s. Note he is carrying both safety lamp and candles. (Stone Collection).

CONTENTS

INTRODUCTION	7
OWNERSHIP OF THE LEAD RIGHTS AND DUTIES	8
THE EARLY HISTORY	9
THE LONDON LEAD COMPANY	9
DERBYSHIRE LEAD ORE	10
EDWARD MILLER WASS AND MILLCLOSE	12
MILLCLOSE COMES OF AGE	13
MILLCLOSE BEFORE THE FIRST WORLD WAR	22
THE END OF AN ERA	29
THE BRADFORD VALE MINING COMPANY AND MILLCLOSE MINES LTD	33
MILLCLOSE IN THE 1920s	35
MILLCLOSE'S LAST FEW YEARS	46
OLD MINERS RECOLLECT THE 1920s AND 1930s	49
THREE CENTURIES OF MINING	59
GLOSSARY	61
ACKNOWLEDGEMENTS	63

Published 1989 by Scarthin Books of Cromford, Derbyshire in conjunction with the Peak District Mines Historical Society Ltd, Peak District Mining Museum, Matlock Bath, Derbyshire.

© Lynn Willies, Keith Gregory, Harry Parker 1989

Printed by Billings & Sons Ltd, Worcester

No part of this book may be reproduced in any form or by any means without the permission of the Owner of the Copyright.

ISBN 0 907758 28 2

2. Plan of the area around Millclose, showing the position of the underground workings. Note they end close by Stanton Hall, not Haddon Hall as many miners believed. The last work at the northern end was done in June 1940. Based on 1923 OS Six Inch Map, and Abandonment Plans (Mining Record Office).

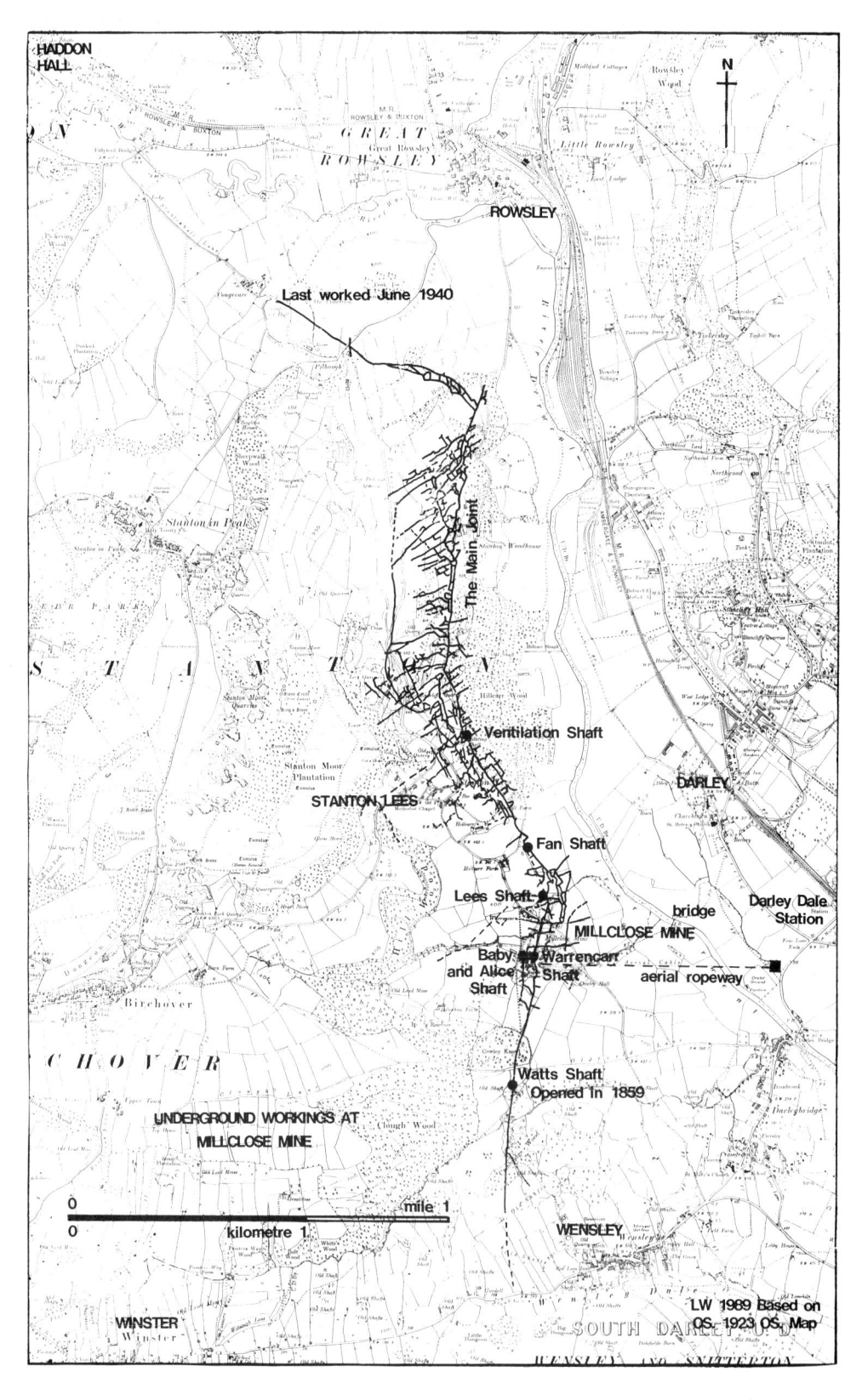

Introduction

THIS IS the story of Millclose Mine, and of the men who worked in it. The site of the mine is near the small, limestone built, mining village of Wensley, close by Darley Dale near Matlock in Derbyshire. In its last and greatest period, it operated for 80 years from 1859 to 1939, when its closure was announced, although it took a further year before it finally stopped and filled with water. At its peak in the 1930s it employed some 800 men, and was the most thoroughly modernised lead mine in the country. Some of the men who worked there remember it almost as if it were yesterday, and there are many contributions here from them.

For local people, and for retired mining engineers in many parts of the world, the mine was and remains almost a legend, with an extremely rich deposit capable of being worked profitably even when the cash price of lead metal was at its lowest for 200 years. Though some men gained wealth from the mine, and many more their livelihoods, the mine took its toll too. This was in more than a few lives, and even more injuries, from explosions, falls of rock, and less spectacularly, from the diseases which result from working in wet conditions and air contaminated by mine gases or smoke from explosives. More than most mines, Millclose suffered from the twin problems of air and water, and its history is dominated by the difficulties they caused and the repeated need to conquer them.

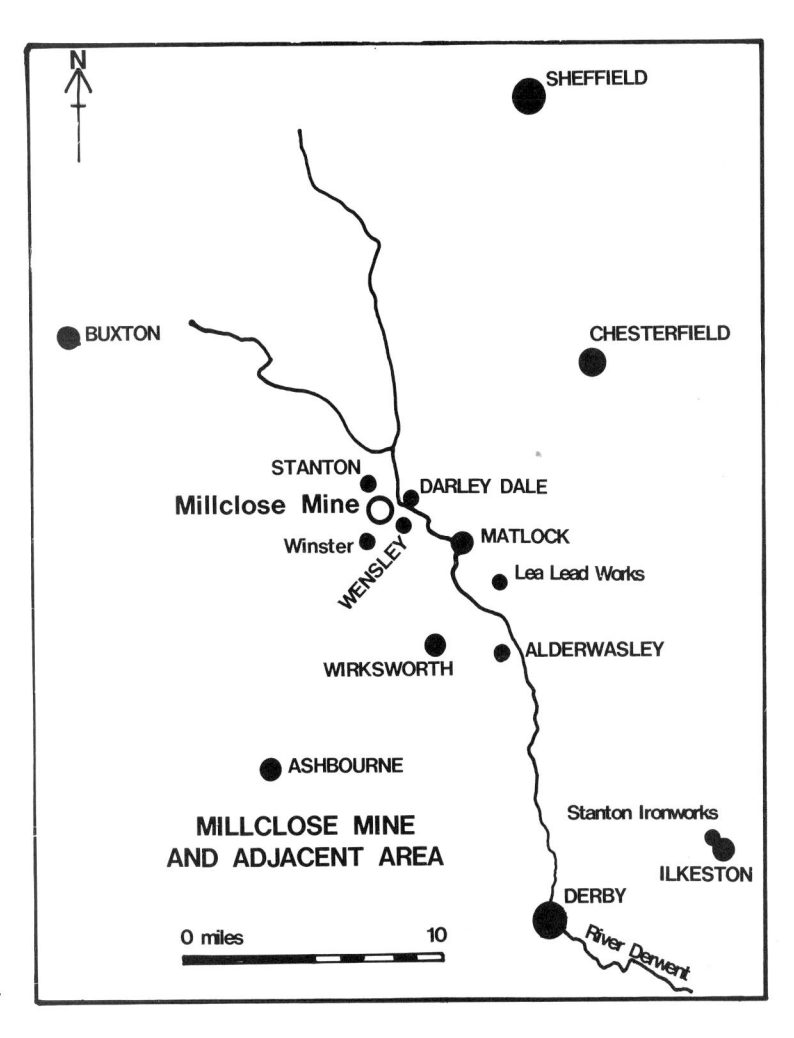

Liberties and Lot

Ownership of the Lead Rights and Duties

THE 17th and 18th century Millclose was almost at the centre of the customary mining Liberty of Wensley, part of the Soke and Wapentake of Wirksworth. (see Glossary, page 61).

This is in the (Kings) Queensfield so that the main duty, lot and cope, would be paid to the Duchy of Lancaster - the ruling monarch's estate, or more accurately, to the lessee or farmer of the duties - Frederick Arkwright in the late 19th century for example. As the mine developed after 1859, the main workings progressed northwards towards the boundary with Stanton, under the flanks of Stanton Moor, and the last freeing dishes of ore were paid to the Wensley barmaster in March 1879.

The Stanton area was more complicated, and not affected by the mining customs. Part of it belonged to the Thornhill family, (Mrs. McCreagh Thornhill in the latter part of the 19th century), part to the Duke of Rutland. Still later, in the 1920s and 30s, it passed into the Rowsley Liberty of the Duke of Rutland. At the boundary areas underground, great care was taken to keep the various ores separate, by careful surveying, and by marking the tubs of ore with one or two wooden pegs for Haddon or Stanton Liberties (waste was indicated by no peg), and at the surface the ore was tipped into separate bins, and dressed separately. The duties or royalties were of course very valuable: in 1929 for instance, a very good year, it is said about £29,000 was paid to the Duke of Rutland.

3. The dressers at Watts Shaft, sometime in the 1880s. Note their curved shovels. Lying on the heap is the wooden dish used for measuring the ore before it was sold. The dish would have been calibrated against the Bronze Dish kept at the Barmoot Court at Wirksworth. Every thirteenth dish was due to the mineral lord, though by that date usually only a twenty-fifth was taken. (PDMHS. Collection).

Rich with much potential

The Early History

THE MINE'S name has an early history, beginning with the working of the mines on the hillside at Wensley, which extended northwards down to the small brook which pours down the valley, and which also bears the name Millclose. These mines are known to have been active in the early 17th century, but the first references to Milnclose Grooves come in the later part of that century, in 1687, when it was said already to be over seventy years old. From the fact that it was considered worthy of protracted dispute, we can guess that it was looked on as rich, with much potential. By that time the workings had penetrated down to the level of the Millclose Brook, and by pumping and bailing of water by hand, probably even deeper: in a rich vein it was not unknown for men to work up to the chest in water, prising the lead ore loose with a bar or gavelock. About 1680 a sough or drainage level began to be driven from lower down the valley, to intersect the Millclose veins, so that after a few years, for the first time it became feasible to work fairly deeply under the river, possibly even under the north side of the brook. Between 1684 and 1687 when the mine was worked "by many hundred peoples" ore worth £10,000 was raised, some 500-600 tons a year. But probably by soon after the turn of the century, the richer ores above water would have become exhausted, and for at least the second time, the mine would have drowned.

No prospect of success

The London Lead Company

THE NEXT phase in its known history was the result of working by the London Lead Company, a company of Quakers known more formally as the "Governor and Company to smelt lead with pit-coal, sea coal". The company had flourished from about 1700 - 1720 in North Wales, and in 1720 expanded its operations to Derbyshire, initially at nearby Winster. At this time Winster was enjoying a considerable boom in mining, especially at the Yatestoop Mine, which was only about half a mile away from Millclose, using the newly invented steam engine for drainage. The Londoners, no doubt to the considerable amusement of knowledgeable locals, were sold mines on Winster Bank which were to prove next to worthless.

From 1743 however they began working Millclose, from a shaft just on the north side of the brook, first using two water wheels, and later also a steam engine to penetrate deep under the shales. From what little we know, or can deduce, it seems likely that although they found enough ore to encourage them for a decade, despite the high costs of steam pumping, they were again not successful. They then transferred their attention to driving a new sough, the Yatestoop Sough, towards Winster, where in 1759 they had taken a share in the Yatestoop Mine. Though a considerable amount of ore was found around 1766 onwards, the profits were small if any, and soon after the Company wound up its affairs, and concentrated on its far more profitable operations in the North Pennines. At Millclose their workings extended some 350 yards north from the brook, to a "forefield shaft" down to depths of some 400 feet below its collar. They used complex pumping arrangements of angle bobs and slide rods to follow the ore along and down, but as before their workings

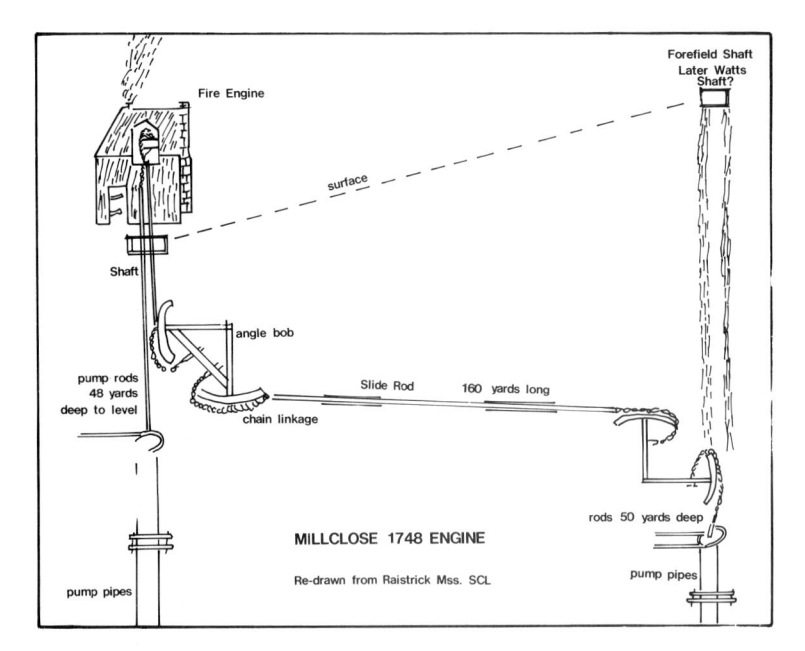

4. The Millclose Engine, as it was drawn in 1748, when the London Lead Company worked the mine. It used a "trail-pump" with rods passing along a level to drain water from a second shaft. The second shaft is probably what later became Watts Shaft. (Raistrick Mss. Sheffield City Library).

5. Watts Shaft Enginehouse about 1880. The giant shear legs were used, with the capstan, right, to raise or lower pumps and timber rods. (Deakin Collection).

finally required hand pumping and bailing. When their steam engine stopped in about 1764 the workings again filled with water, and probably remained so for the best part of a century, when the final phase began which lasted until 1939. In the minute book of the Company, for September 1764, it was recorded, "Millclose Mine, Derbyshire, has been effectively tried under level and there is no prospect of success".

Not found at depth

Derbyshire Lead Ore

THE LEAD ore, mainly galena, found in Derbyshire mines is usually at its richest where the limestone passes underneath the overlying shale. This was the situation at Millclose. At the village of Wensley the limestone is found at surface, but northwardly it slopes steeply down, and but for the valley of the brook, would be very deep indeed. Of course north of the brook it once again gets deeper for a while, but gradually the limestone levels out under what became the later mine at Warren Carr, and a little further north even rises again. The lead ore, often with some zinc ore, called blende, with other minerals such as fluorspar, barite and calcite, is found in both fissure veins, filling natural joints or faults in the rock, and in pipes - old cave systems which form a network of interconnecting passages which have been infilled with minerals.

At Millclose the ore was also found in flats, wide thin areas, usually at the base of the shales, in a zone as much as several hundred feet wide, and sometimes very rich indeed. Often groundwaters had flowed through the fissure and pipe systems, dissolving away some of the minerals, and sometimes naturally concentrating the heavy lead ore on the floor of caverns, where it could be removed with no more than picks and shovels. Most Derbyshire lead deposits were and are fairly shallow, though a few mines have found ore at depth. Before 1859, when Millclose re-opened, there had been a number of failures where companies had sunk deep into the limestone and in some cases through volcanic beds of lava, known locally as toadstones. Millclose was to prove that in fact the prevailing belief that ore was not found at depth was wrong on both counts: first when ore was found deep under the shales, and later, after 1929, when even larger amounts of lead and zinc ores were found under not just one, but several toadstones down to a total depth of about 1010 feet. When we marvel at the richness of the Millclose deposit, and the profits made from it we should also remember the scores of other mines which failed, and the losses made on them. For mining investors the risk was very high indeed: it was an adventure.

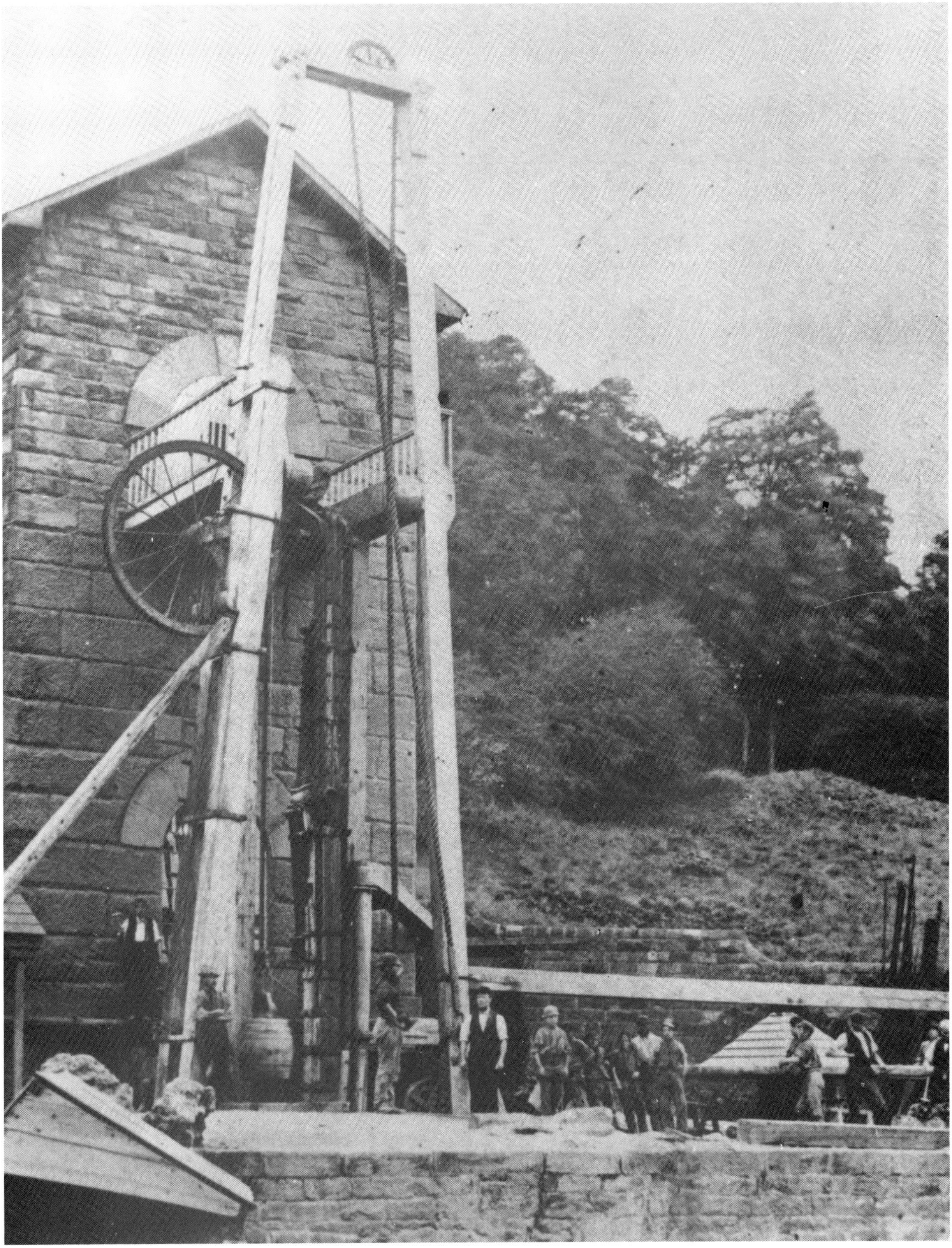

Hang on 'til you find cow

Edward Miller Wass and Millclose

6. Watts Shaft showing also the steam winder. On the right are the hutches or hand jigs. The top-hatted gentlemen, left, is said to be E.M. Wass, who died in 1886. (Deakin Collection).

ACCORDING TO repute, Wass, the owner of a lead smelter at Lea, a few miles away, had already by 1859 lost some £75,000 of his own money in other lead mines, and in the opinion of most investors, Derbyshire was a worked out field. Most felt the old Millclose had been thoroughly tried by the London Lead Company in the middle years of the 18th century. On the other hand, Wass recorded that it was said that not only had the old vein been rich to the last, but that a "draw" of rich ore would be found ready broken, which the miners had not been allowed time to bring to the surface. There was no such ore.

In 1859, what became known as Watts Shaft (see fig.2 - it is also shown as Capstan Shaft on the OS 25 inch map) was reopened by Wass, near the most northerly and deepest part of the old workings, down through the shales to the limestone ore-bearing beds some 300 feet below the collar. A fifty inches diameter cylinder Cornish steam engine, at 80 Horse Power far more powerful than that of a century earlier, was bought from Thornewill and Warham of Burton-on-Trent, and erected in 1860. It had pumps of sixteen inches diameter. The House was very handsomely built of massive gritstone blocks, and to the west side of it was placed a steam winder, made by the same company. Photographs show also a large man-operated capstan, which would have been used to lower pump rods and pipes. Work commenced by the driving of a long level southwards, deep under the old workings for over a quarter-mile, roughly to under the Wensley-Winster road. Because the rocks dipped towards the mine, the level was able to pass through a toadstone, into the "second limestone" beneath. Very little ore was found.

Wass then directed his miners to drive northwardly, and by the mid 1860s, the level had reached Warren Carr, about a half mile north from the original shaft, and close by the boundary of Wensley with Stanton. This time very rich ore was found, though according to one source, only after the available capital had all been used, and the miners had volunteered to continue work for nothing. Wass said the main vein was extraordinarily large, "seldom less than ten yards wide", and sometimes so wide twenty or thirty men could work abreast. In 1872 one such cavity or flat was worked for a width of eighty yards, with forty-two men producing 200 tons of dressed lead ore a month from it. With the exception of a very few years, from this time, Millclose was Derbyshire's major producer. The ore was found just beneath the shale, and a major problem was fire damp or methane. The gas sometimes used to spurt out, making a noise like a singing-kettle, and the miners are said to have set light to it, using it for illumination. This was of course extremely dangerous, though less so than in coal mining, where the dust was combustible, adding a thousand times more fuel to any explosion.

Jumbo, Baby, and Alice

Millclose Comes of Age

THE OLD ENEMY was of course water, and as the mine grew, and more ground was laid open, so the inflow increased. All the water was brought back along the level to Watts Shaft, and in late 1874 an inrush caused work in the mine to cease for almost two years. The problem had been anticipated, and at Warren Carr a fifty fathom (300 feet) deep shaft had been sinking in readiness. From this time, Warren Carr was to become the main focus of activity, though Watts Shaft remained in use until about 1889. On this shaft a new engine, "Jumbo", was erected, which had an eighty-inch cylinder, one of the most powerful in the country, and made by the famous firm of Harvey and Co. of Hayle in Cornwall. It was a 250 to 300 Horse Power engine, with four large Galloway boilers and pumps of 24 inches diameter.

These raised nearly 180 gallons per stroke, with, about 1880, three and a half strokes per minute. The mine water was raised 36 fathoms into the Yatestoop Sough, which is some 64 feet below surface, and was clearly one of the reasons for locating the shaft here. By June 1877 the two engines were coping easily again with the water, and there was said to be much spare capacity with Jumbo, probably double that in use, in case of flood. Two other new shafts were also sunk nearby, since it was apparent the richest ore occurred in this area.

At Stanton Lees, a few hundred yards away at the furthest extent of the workings, a new ventilation shaft was made. In November 1887 an explosion led to this shaft having a fan installed, the first major mechanical mine ventilation system in a Derbyshire lead mine.

7. Part of the 1883 mechanised dressing floors. Two rotary buddles are visible, probably out of a total of five, and behind them, right, are wooden jigs. The buddles still had to be dug out, hence the wheel-barrows, and were replaced in 1899. (Morgan Collection).

This followed criticism by the Mines Inspector A.H. Stokes, and led to adoption of "The Special Rules", which meant safety lamps had to be used in gassy places, though candles - tallow dips, were used in areas away from the shales. To save ore and waste being trammed back to the older Watts Shaft, about 800 yards along a narrow level, a new oval winding shaft of about 11 x 8 feet in size was also sunk, to 50 fathoms, called Lees Shaft. This was the largest shaft on the mine, and in 1886 was operated by a portable engine, with a winding drum attached, but was soon after fitted with a permanent winder with two cages from Watts Shaft.

Previously of course all ore had emerged via Watts Shaft. Photographs show the top of this to have been very crowded, with climbing, winding, and pumping all taking place in it. Ore when brought out, after crushing, was treated by hand, by picking out good pieces, and by jigging or buddling the rest: some hand jigs or hutches can be seen in the photograph. These used a counterbalanced arm to plunge a sieve in water. Jigging the sieve caused the heavy ore to settle on the wires, with waste above, so they could be separated. It was heavy work, though skilful. As part of the changes, Wass introduced the first properly mechanised dressing floor into Derbyshire, completed in 1883. There had been a visit to the mine in 1880 by the Midland Counties Institution of Mining Engineers, who had convinced Wass of the merit of converting to full mechanisation, and soon after the equipment was supplied by the Sandicroft Foundry, and worked well after a year or so of teething problems. In 1878 over 3300 tons of dressed ore had been produced at the mine - one of the largest amounts of high quality ore in a year of any Derbyshire mine to that time. In 1887, with mechanised floors, it was claimed to be 60% cheaper, and 3% more effective at removing the lead ore, and output had risen to almost 4000 tons. This was some 85% of all ore raised in Derbyshire, and 8% of that in Britain. Some zinc ore was also produced, which would have been extremely difficult to separate by hand methods. Power for the dressing operations was provided by a steam engine. The main

By instructions from the Devisees in Trust for sale under the Wills of the late

Mrs. ANNE WASS, of The Green, Lea, in the parish of Ashover in the County of Derby, and of the late EDWARD M. WASS, of Matlock Bath, in the same County, Esquire.

8. Notice of the sale of Millclose, 1886, following Wass' death. It was not sold. (Derbyshire Record Office, Stone and Symons Collection).

Particulars and Conditions

OF SALE OF VERY VALUABLE

LEAD MINING AND OTHER REAL & LEASEHOLD ESTATES

In the parishes of Wensley, Wirksworth, Crich, and elsewhere, in the County of Derby,

INCLUDING THE CELEBRATED LEAD MINE KNOWN AS THE

MILL CLOSE STOOP OR MILL CLOSE MINE,

Situate in the parishes or townships of Stanton-le-Peak, Birchover, & Wensley-cum-Snitterton,

AND ALSO OF

SHARES IN COMPANIES,

Which will be offered for Sale by Public Auction,

BY

MR. GEORGE MARSDEN,

At the "NEW BATH" HOTEL, MATLOCK BATH,

On *THURSDAY*, the 11th day of *NOVEMBER*, 1886,

At TWO o'clock in the Afternoon (for THREE o'clock precisely,)

unless previously disposed of by private contract, and either altogether or in the following or such other lots as shall be determined upon at the time of sale, and subject to conditions of sale to be then produced.

It is proposed to offer Lots 1 to 26, both inclusive, and Lot 28 as one Lot.

For particulars & conditions of sale, and for further information, apply to Messrs. F. and H. TAYLOR, Solicitors, Bakewell; the AUCTIONEER, Wirksworth, Derby; or to

MEE & CO.,

SOLICITORS, RETFORD, NOTTS.

October, 1886.

HODSON, PRINTER, RETFORD.

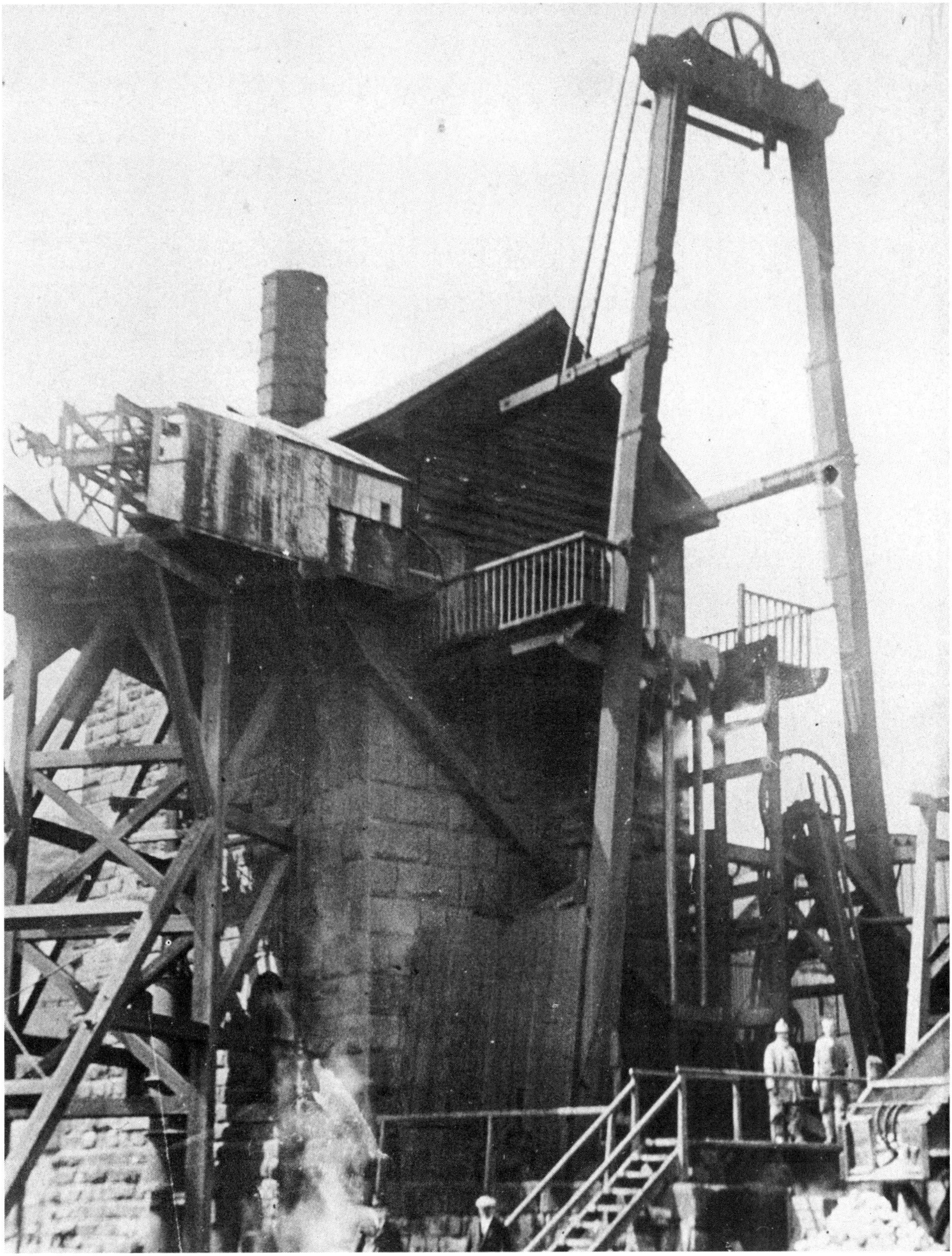

9. The "Jumbo" engine house, with its tall shear legs, and showing the aerial ropeway possibly in the course of erection, in 1912. Jumbo was an 80 inch engine of, in 1921, 277 HP, raising 1416 gallons per minute from 466.7 feet. Unusually, it had a form of parallel motion on the outdoor side, with a crosshead running in slides just below the shaft top, to which the pump rods were connected. This, probably erroneously, was said to enable the engine to work faster. (Frank Brindley, British Speleological Association Collection, BCRA).

10. The "Baby and Alice" engines, indoors. The two cylinders are visible, with Baby on the left. (Edgar Brook, PDMHS Bulletin).

11. Baby (right) and Alice outdoors. Note the shear leg, and left, a small pipe bringing in the "house water", used for condensing the steam. The pumps discharged 64 feet lower, into Yatestoop Sough. (Stone Collection).

features of the new process were the use of a Blake-Marsden Crusher, which discharged on to a picking table where good ore and useless waste could immediately be removed. From there the ore passed through trommels - rotating sieves - with the larger pieces again crushed using rolls. It was then classified into various sizes, and treated in jigs or round buddles. When separated the ore was taken by horse and cart to the Lea Lead Works, a distance of about 8 miles, where it was smelted.

Edward Miller Wass, son of Joseph Wass a lead smelter, had been born in Holloway near Lea in 1829, and was educated at the Anthony Gell School in Wirksworth. He had taken over his father's business in 1852, and as well as maintaining the smelting business, vigorously went into mining also, not just for lead, but also clay and coal at Meerbrook, Alderwasley. When he died in 1886, and was buried in Darley Churchyard, according to report "his own workmen assembled in great numbers, and strong and stalwart miners quivered and wept like delicately nurtured women as the remains of the master were lowered to their last resting place." The mine was then at a peak of production and efficiency, and his family decided on a sale of all his mining and smelting property, including shares in hundreds of small mines, a few larger, and of course his wholly owned Millclose. However at the 11th November sale at the New Bath Hotel at Matlock Bath, insufficient bids were made, and the Wass Trustees remained in control until 1919, when the mine was finally sold to the Bradford Vale Mining Company.

In 1896 Cyril Parsons, a visiting mining engineer, described the mine. By then it was working a mostly vertical fissure which varied from a few inches to twenty feet wide. Sometimes it was filled with a mass of broken material, at other places it had "ribs" of zinc blende, fluorspar and barytes, galena (lead ore) and calcite, with sometimes at its centre, a solid band of fools gold, iron pyrite, a foot thick. Where it opened into a cavity, there were splendid masses of cubical galena and dog-tooth calcite. There were many colourful but minor minerals, and large quantities of brown ochreous mud, formed from decomposing pyrite. Caverns were found, often unexpectedly, mainly by following veins on the western side, or along the main vein. They could measure as much as sixty feet in all directions, with masses of ore and other materials on the floor, big enough in some cases to provide work for years. Out of such discoveries, made by following a thin leader of ore, came one of the miners' aphorisms: "when you find tail, hang on 'til you find cow", and it was never more true than at Millclose.

In 1887 the Warren Carr Shaft was deepened, probably to 73 fathoms, and a new lift of

12. The Lees Shaft winding engine, made by Thornewill and Warham, in 1860. "It was certainly of historical interest" said one who rode it regularly. It had several drivers, including John Wild, "King" of the Winster Morris men. (Edgar Brook, William Else Collection).

plunger pumps were installed. The engines then coped with about 1000 gallons a minute. This was about 6500 tons of water a day - day in, day out. Two years later a new shaft had been sunk a short distance from Warren Carr, and a curious and probably unique enginehouse built. This housed two engines, "Baby", the old engine from Watts Shaft, and "Alice" another older engine, brought from Wakebridge Mine at Crich, which had also been owned by Wass. These pumped water from the 50 fathom level, with one acting as standby. Watts Shaft was of course no longer used except as part of the ventilation system. At the time of Parson's visit, yet another shaft was sinking, 600 yards further north from the Fan Shaft, at the furthermost extent of the mine then. When completed, the use of the old Fan Shaft was given up, and the fan, or possibly a new fan was put on the new shaft, usually known as the ventilation shaft. Rather surprisingly the fan blew air into the mine, rather than extracted it, as would have been more usual. The reason for this was that large quantities of water poured down the shaft, helping force air into the mine, and out through the other shafts.

Once away from the steam engines and pumps, and the winder on the Lees Shaft, everything was still done entirely by hand. Where the rock or vein was strong, then holes were hand drilled by "beating the borer", either single handed, or by a two man team. In other cases a pick and shovel were sufficient, the ore and waste being loaded into tubs on a narrow gauge track to be hand trammed back to the shaft. Where possible the drives - the access tunnels -followed the twists and turns in the vein, though cross cuts were made to explore for parallel veins or to move ore between them. Ideally ore was broken out of the vertical fissures in stopes by overhand methods, so that after blasting it fell, or could

13. Lighting the fuses, using candles, early this century. (Stone Collection).

easily be moved, by gravity into chutes down to one of three haulage levels: the main level at 50 fathoms, another at 42 fathoms, and the "shale gateway", north of Lees Shaft, at about 36 fathoms. But the nature of the smaller side veins was such as sometimes to need work below the level, so that ore had to be wound up using a hand windlass. Where possible too, any waste rock was stored below ground, in the empty stopes or caverns, once the ore had been cleared out.

Regrettably, relatively little is known in detail of the people involved at Millclose in the late 19th century. Even E.M. Wass largely remains an enigmatic figure. He probably at first took a very active part in managing the mine, but by 1878 had appointed Joseph Greatorex as the Mine Manager - he held the post for ten years, at a time of greatly expanding output, and over the period of Wass' death: on retirement he was awarded a magnificent gold watch. He was succeeded by A.M. Alsop - their family had long associations with lead mining and smelting, and had been close aquaintances of the Wass family. Alsop was also the Barmaster for the Soke and Wapentake of Wirksworth, and held both posts for many years. The Chief Engineer was Cornish, Captain Stephen Thomas, and came from Leedstown near Hayle to install Jumbo and its pumps in 1877: others were Cornish too. Most of the men were of course local, from Darley and Darley Bridge, from Wensley and Winster, and a few from further afield, such as Cumberland. They walked to work - from Wensley a well made gritstone slabbed path made the passage over the muddy shales easier. Today it is deeply hollowed by the passing of thousands of clog-irons. From Winster they followed the footpath down to and along the Millclose Brook.

Millclose Mine still operated the traditional bargain system for most of the miners. Every few weeks, usually six or seven, the manager agreed a contract with teams of miners to carry out work, though wages were paid for work like firing boilers, or for enginemen. The teams, known as "companies" varied in size, and both they and often the place they worked in were called after the leading man, eg. Bateman's Company, Bateman's Winze etc. The bargains varied in type, but the two most common were where the amount paid directly related to the amount of the ore got, and secondly a bargain for driving, sometimes called "fathomtail", used in drilling and blasting through rock, and paid by the fathom driven of an agreed size. They supplied, or at least paid for their own powder, tools and candles. The team or company was typically about a dozen strong, divided between the three shifts, but might be larger or smaller as the work demanded. Usually the amount earned was greater than for day-work, with the possibility of very high sums if an unexpectedly rich ore-body was found, matched by the risk of it being unexpectedly poor. Companies of miners often worked together at the mine for many years. In all there were generally about 100-150 men working underground, and about half as many at surface. Underground shifts were six hours long, though it was common to work overtime, and frequently double shifts, whilst surface workers worked up to twelve hours, six days a week.

A Mining Revolution

Millclose Before the First World War

THE TURN OF the century and the years up to the First World War saw further developments, which seem to have been the particular responsibility of Daniel Morgan, whose photographs are an important feature in this book. He remained at the mine until 1922, and his son Elias looked after the steam engines even later. Anthony Alsop died in 1907 or thereabouts, and L.C. Stuckey took over as Manager, writing his own account of the mine in 1917. The major improvements seem to have been around 1900, and then just before the War.

In 1899 the dressing floors were again modernised, and improved and faster jigs for coarse ore were introduced, whilst for the finer ores, the earlier round buddles seen in photograph 7 were supplemented, and eventually replaced by the recently invented Wilfley Tables. In 1914 these were in turn replaced by improved Deister Tables. The tables treated fine grained particles of ore extremely well, continuously rather than in

14. A James Table, and blocks for another, about 1936. The older, either Wilfley or Deister Tables can be seen in the rear. They replaced the earlier round buddles for treating slimes. (Stone collection).

batches like the round buddles they replaced. They worked by giving a suspended table a series of sharp side movements, whilst ore was passed in a thin slurry over a surface fitted with small riffles. The ore separated according to the various specific gravities, and poured in streams over different parts of the edge, to be caught in launders and run off for dewatering. Such tables were especially effective, by the standards of the day, at separating zinc from lead. Zinc, once considered a menace because of the difficulty of separating it from the lead ore, was becoming more and more important, and was used for galvanising, as for the "wriggly tin" sheets used on roofs. The mine using the jigs also produced some barites, used by the paint industry of which there were more than a dozen small works locally, and some calcite which was used for "spar-dashing" of houses, and as a gravel for paths etc.

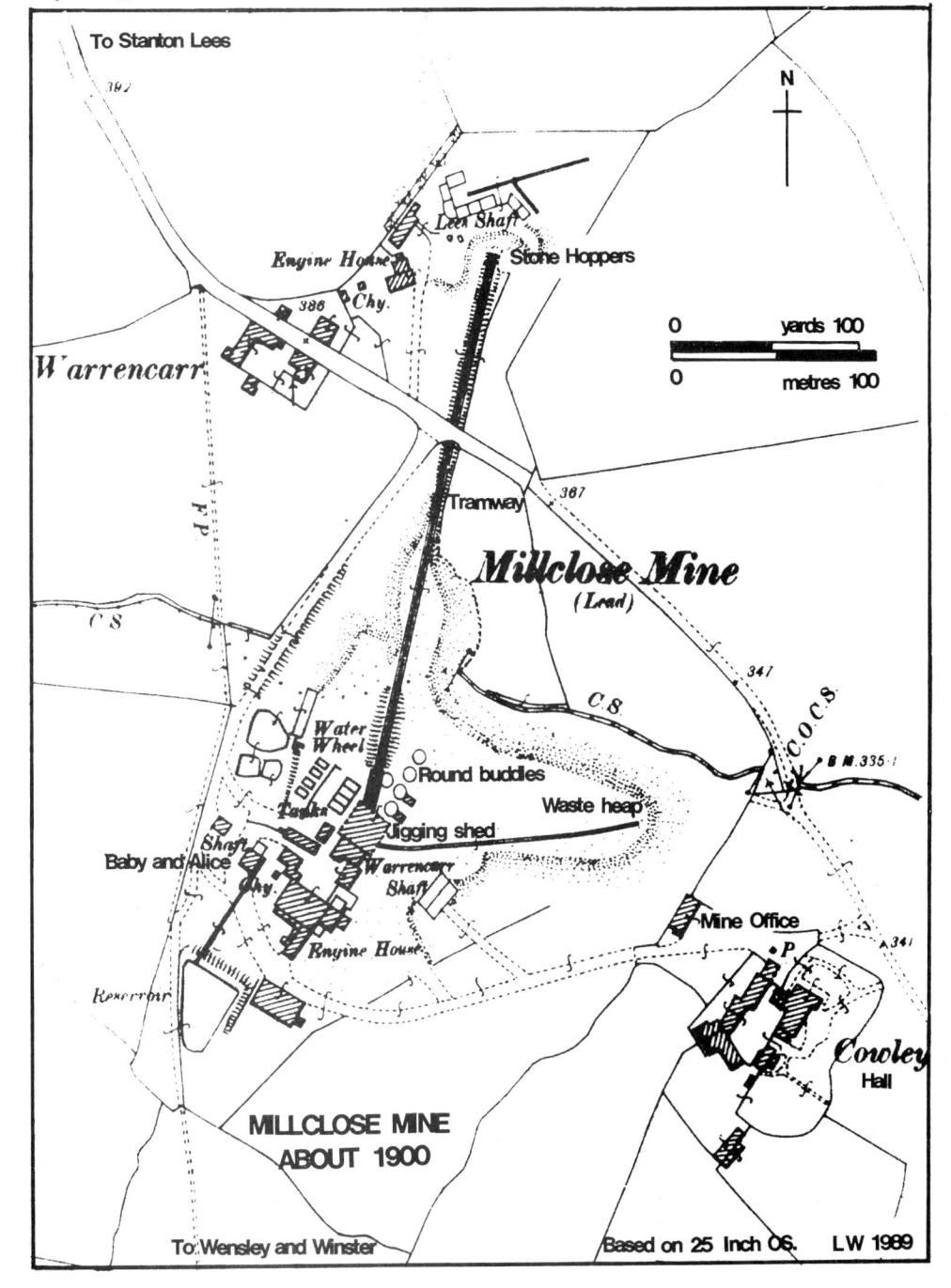

15. Millclose about 1900, based on the 1905 OS. 25 inch map, showing the main shafts and the linking tramway. The round buddles were probably removed about this time.

16. A "dolly tub", used to separate very fine grained material as a final operation. (Stone Collection).

In 1901 the Lees Shaft was sunk to 73 fathoms. This probably marked the successful development of the 73 fathom level (this is also sometimes referred to as the 70 fathom) following the deepening of Warren Carr and setting up of Baby and Alice a decade earlier. For both ventilation and drainage this would have needed to be developed for a long distance before systematic stoping could begin, though doubtless some ore was got as it was driven. Whereas the 50 fathom level used a rail gauge of about 12 inches, the deeper level was larger, with waggons running on a 17 inch gauge track. Most of the work done getting ore from this level before 1914 was south of the Lees Shaft, and it was not until nearly 1914 that work started in earnest on the north side, and because of the toadstone found at the Lees shaft, this had to be north of the Ventilation Shaft where the measures had dipped down again. In the ten years up to the end of 1913, the mine averaged 4500 tons of lead ore concentrate and 308 tons of blende annually, yielding a handsome profit for those days of about £28,200 per year.

The most obvious of the surface improvements was the aerial ropeway, then very fashionable on mines, made by Bullivants and which led across from the mine, from the side of the Jumbo Engine House, over the river to a field known as Old Hay, next to the road at Darley Cricket Field, a short distance from the railway. A suspension bridge was probably put in across the river at the same date, possibly to facilitate maintenance, but it was even more convenient for the Darley footpath. It seems to have been an extravagant way to save a mile of cartage, as coal had to be brought to the ropeway terminal by horse and cart from the station, probably since the coal merchant, Tom Wright, had an exclusive agreement, or ownership of the intervening land. It carried some 10-12 tons of coal per hour up to the mine, and 20 tons of gravel (calcite) away, for a distance of just over 1000 yards. It needed two men to handle, load, and discharge the buckets via chutes at either end. The photographs of the period also suggest the arrangements for transfering ore from the Lees Shaft, where it was raised, to the mill were also improved. New hoppers, rather like huge limekilns were built of stone to take 300 tons of ore near the shaft, and a cutting made to allow waggons to run under the hoppers. The waggons, two up, two down, were drawn from Lees Shaft, under the road, by steam powered, rope-hauled tramway, dumping directly into the crusher bin, close by Jumbo Shaft.

Even more revolutionary was the adoption of electricity and wider use of compressed air. A new power-house was built, to house a generator made by Bellis Morcom-Westinghouse of 150 kw capacity. The main use of this was to power new electric centrifugal pumps, made by Mather and Platt and installed on the 73 fathom level at Lees Shaft, pumping 1800 gallons of water a minute up to the 50 fathom level. Jumbo pumped some water direct to surface still from 73 fathoms, and some also to the 50 fathom.

17. Crushing calcite gravel. It is possibly Ben Walker of Cross Green. (Stone Collection).

18. Millclose Mine 1924-27, showing the aerial ropeway at Warrencarr (Jumbo) Shaft, possibly about to be demolished: other photos show the timbers in the foreground and no ropeway. (HMP Collection).

19. The Ropeway or "flight" crossing the Stanton Lees road. It was 3064 feet long, electrically powered, and ended near the present Darley Dale cricket field, carrying coal to the mine, and calcite gravel back. (Stone Collection).

20. The 30 feet high Lees Shaft headgear, with two seven feet diameter pulleys. Ore was pushed in tubs from the shaft, and tipped into two 300 ton stone hoppers, then drawn via the tramway to the dressing floor at Warrencarr Shaft. (Stone Collection).

21. The 300 yard long rope-hauled inclined tramway to Warrencarr Shaft. Probably about 1923. The smoking chimney has a 1905 datestone, and is still standing. (Stone Collection).

22. The main underground pumping station, on the 70 fathom level, first installed about 1912, but seen here about 1930. (Stone Collection).

23. "Proctors New Patent" mechanical stoker, claimed to be 25% more efficient than hand stoking, firing a total of four Galloway boilers. The photograph is one of a stereo pair, possibly pre 1914. (Morgan Collection).

24. "Green's Economiser" - 288 tubes in three batteries, with scrapers driven by an engine in the Jumbo house. It used waste heat in the smoke on its way to the chimney to pre-heat boiler feed water. In course of construction about 1912, it was later arched over. The figure is possibly Daniel Morgan. (Morgan Collection).

From 50 fathoms, Baby, the 50 inch engine pumped to the sough, with Alice kept on standby. Obviously the water problems were growing, and of course the engines were far from new: the average amount of water to be pumped by the beginning of the War was approaching 1800 gallons a minute, and the new pumps could handle greater than usual inflows, and cope with breakdowns or maintenance. The generator also provided power for the aerial ropeway, using a motor made by John Davis of Derby, and incandescent lighting was installed at the 73 fathom shaft station and pumping station.

This was of course far in advance of most other mines, even many large coal mines, and long before the public supply came to the area. The generator, and the Schramm Compressor (probably supplied by Markham's of Chesterfield), were powered by steam engines with steam from a new set of boilers. These also were very modern, and used coal slack fed by automatic stokers. A Green's Economiser, seen in photograph 24 in the course of being erected, was used to pre-heat the boiler feed water using waste heat from the flue gases. By the onset of war, Millclose was probably the best equipped metal mine in the country. Capable of producing as much as ever, and with better prices, Millclose entered another period of prosperity. Production in the five years to the end of 1918 was a little lower than pre-war, at 3400 tons of lead concentrate a year, and 400 tons of blende, but profits on average were only a little down, at £27,800 a year. Since these averaged figures seem to be all that were available at the sale soon after, we might expect they do in fact mask falling production near the end of the war.

Petty jealousies and pent-up feelings

The End of an Era

BY 1918 THE mine was looking jaded. It had never been worked in such a way as to have large reserves blocked out, but generally it was not difficult to find a workable prospect in one of the hundreds of leaders - thin veinlets, that so frequently had led on to new deposits. The 73 fathom level had cut through a toadstone around Lees Shaft, but had found better ground north of the new Fan Shaft, but this was largely worked out. Money had also been obtained from the Ministry of Munitions to test the limestone under the toadstone further north - via an underground shaft or winze, known thereafter as the Munitions Winze, but to no avail. The mine was also involved in a protracted dispute with some of its workforce, involving some five strikes and/or lockouts, between 1917 and 1919. Since lead mining seems to have had only two previous strikes, one in the 1770s, and the next in the 1860s, this was a major social change.

Some of the workforce, feeling under pressure because of wartime inflation, and following the imposition of eight hour shifts ten weeks earlier, had formed a branch of the Derbyshire Miners Association at Winster, the first time the miners' union had recruited in the local lead industry. As the Union put it, "It was the utter helplessness of the men, their low starvation wages, longer hours, and the increased cost of living" which of course contrasted with the enrichment of the owners. The Winster President was John Millward. In mid August 1917 he and Frank Hall, J.P., of the Miners' Association had presented the Company with a demand including either longer contracts, of six months, or a day wage. Major Denman, the principal of the two Wass Trustees, and Mr Stuckey the mine manager refused this vigorously. They would only accept a day wage below that necessary for a comfortable living, by local standards, because of the problem of supervision, and certainly would not give a 50% increase based on the last bargains, but would agree to a 46 hour week, provided that a return to six hour shifts was at three quarters the wage of an eight hour shift. They would agree to bargains being made by three men for each team, one from each shift, and considered that bargain periods of six or seven weeks were as long as was fair to proprietors and men. Higher wages Denman said would necessarily mean the weeding out of all inefficient labour, so that no workman could look upon himself as permanently employed.

According to the Derbyshire Times, unless a settlement was arrived at, the government would take over the mine. The owners also put out a notice of wages paid at the last bargain end:

". . . . . wages earned over the ten weeks covered by the extension to eight hours . . . . . to men who work full time to eleven shifts of six hours . . . . . to Saturday July 28, 1917. Mosley's Company £2-15-3 per week six shifts, Stone's Company £2-3-1, Taylor's Company £3-2-5, Goodall's £2-2-6, Gratton's Company £2-4-8, Bateman's Company £2-6-7, Ingman's £2-3-11". A correspondent added, "the men have been well paid" (£1-5-0 would have been a reasonable agricultural wage - and probably others at the mine earned no more), "and it must not be forgotten either that these men mostly have other occupations besides mining, many of them being small farmers, and others shopkeepers, so that their earnings at the mine have been augmented considerably in other ways". Certainly this was true of the Batemans, who lived in Winster, whose family kept two, three or more cows, sold some milk to local people, and also via the dairy at Rowsley Station. Subsequently the miners went back to work, but three weeks later, at the end of a short bargain to allow negotiations, they struck again, but after a few days were back at work.

In September 1918 the Miners' Association asked the Minister of Munitions to intervene, and a strike was only narrowly averted, when after the mine management had refused to

25. Topping out a new chimney, next to Baby and Alice shaft, probably after repairs. The date is uncertain, but probably c1912. The long ladders are a feature of several photographs. (Morgan Collection).

accept an arbitration award, the Minister was again involved. A letter of October 1918 gives a brief glimpse of the affairs at the mine, and of the unprecedented intervention by government in mining and industry generally. The letter was from John Saxton, a mining engineer from Mallin Bridge, Sheffield. He had obvious sympathies with the Miners' Association, and was called in to give advice on the situation at Millclose. He refers to a Mr Collins, the Ministry of Production's engineer with responsibility for the mine. He commented on the general run of the ore in the mine as not being good - only moderate, and that lead mining was speculative - for men and master, who could not see beyond the blow of a pick or depth of a drill. He felt there was fair scope for bargains to be let - obviously the old system of sub-contracting work to companies was still in place - and suggested five possible places:

"1. Bateman's: Both north and south in a cavity, from which an ore pass should be cut to the bottom level. (This was almost certainly Sam Bateman from Winster. His father had worked at the mine and his sons Sam and Bill also worked there in the 1930s. He was leader of a company of miners).

2. H (arold) Bargh's place: (Daniel) Ingmans Coy. Here there was good prospect by following a wet hole along the water line (this must have been on the 73 fathom level).

3. Moseley's. There was a good show of ore under some big lumps, but the small blocks were said to be more dangerous than the large. A strut or bridge should be left in (as protection).

4. Goodall's Drive, Taylor's section: There was the beginning of a leader (ie a narrow veinlet of mineral, leading, it was hoped, to better). It was suggested a leak of compressed air would ventilate the blind heading.

5. Baum's (Boam's?) Drive. Open out on a promising leader in the roof and stope to Black Bed. (This would either be at the north end of the 73 fathom level, or higher in the workings near the main shafts, just under the shale)".

In all he felt there was sufficient work for thirty men breaking and loading, plus waggoners.

Saxton felt further efficiency might be gained by putting horses to work on the 70 fathom level, with the waggoners put on leading and waggoning to the ore pass, that is, pushing the tubs from smaller work places to the main level, probably relieving the miners of this job. There is no indication this was done, and indeed would have been very expensive due to the need to build stables etc. But mechanised haulage on this level followed a very few years later.

He had particular advice about the need to develop good labour relations. There were "peculiar methods of payments", ie the traditional bargain system, "old servants and length of service", petty jealousies and other matters which had grown up in an old family mine, made worse by lack of other work in the area for men with a grievance, "causing spirited miners to think a good deal, say nothing, and lose efficiency". He went on later to say that old customs and expectations must die out, and petty jealousies and pent-up feelings also. "I must impress upon you that each and every man must put out all his best work and skill for all parties concerned, and it would be better for all your officials to impress this thoroughly on the workmen at a mass meeting". Good advice, and quite clearly Saxton was aware of the pressures on the mine and its management, but it was not necessarily palatable to the union.

For coal miners of course the war and government intervention in coal and iron mines had made for great political awareness, and there were great hopes for nationalisation of coal mines. It seems unlikely that the Millclose miners had similar aims, and even less likely the government had for lead mining. The reasons were predominantly local - though the attempted solutions were nationally politically fashionable. For some of them it was an awareness that the old, deferential society was changing about them - and there was an unwillingness, a stubbornness perhaps, to accept that the mine and mining was changing too.

26. Raithe Mine, Elton, about 1920, showing Millclose "strikers", who set up their own mining company in conjunction with the Derbyshire Miners Association. Left to right: A. Fengls, A. Naydon, C. Stone, R.Stone, A. Goodwin, B.Slack, W. Walker, Bill Haywood, John Millward, and front, W. Stone. (John Millward Collection).

In all during 1918 - 1919, there were five strikes. The last of these, it was claimed , resulted from the closure of a number of working places in late July, with the transfer of non-union men to the workplaces of those in the union, and the sacking, on the grounds there was no work for them, of trade union members, some of whom had worked at Millclose for many years. The union wanted non-unionists to be dismissed first, and then the last to have been employed, which was not acceptable. As a result the union threatened to withdraw the stokers, (intending it was later claimed, not to flood the mine, but to prevent men being wound down). The owners then posted a notice, ". . . . . so that stokers intending to obey the order for withdrawal are requested to state hereon by noon tomorrow the last shift each is prepared to work so as to enable the management to have ready his pay up to the time of his leaving". Subsequently, in September, following the dismissal of eight men, 84 men, probably not all members of the union, came out on strike.

The proprietors on the 24th October increased wages by the full 50% previously denied, "now that the members of the Derbyshire Miners' Association have ceased to be employed . . . . . in recognition of the improved efficiency of the work above and below ground", and invited their employees to join with them in a "pit welfare committee". They were convinced that "good will come out of past evil . . . . . now that efficiency and contentment have replaced the sulky slacking of the past 2 years".

The dispute so far as the union was concerned was still unsettled in November, and the union informed the Minister of Labour that they were considering a strike ballot of all their members. They also decided to investigate helping the Winster men to form a mining cooperative, and a "nicking " of three mines was organised with the Barmaster. This is the ancient custom whereby mines out of workmanship can be claimed by miners wishing to work them, at negligible expense. Meanwhile the strike was terminated when the mine was sold to the Bradford Vale Mining Co. at the end of the year, and a bitter-sweet twist was added by Denman, according to the Derbyshire Times, awarding those miners at work at the mine a £10,000 bonus - a very considerable sum amongst probably some two to three hundred men.

Since however the new owners also said they could not re-employ the miners, the union proceeded with its cooperative scheme. At the end of February, some £1000 had been expended on the dispute, and a further £200 had been spent on the proposed development. Further money was found from the balance of a wartime ambulance fund, and again John Saxton the Sheffield Mining Engineer was called in to give an expert opinion. He, as mining engineers in those days were wont to do (and sometimes nowadays too), gave a glowing opinion of the prospects, and in May the Raithe Lead-Mining Company Ltd. was set up to work the mine, at Elton, just behind the church. It had a nominal capital of £7000, though despite appeals to the coal miner members of the Association only about £1000 was raised. Amongst the seven directors were John Millward of Winster, William Harwood of Elton, and Andrew Nedin of Winster. Their objective was to drive westwardly from what had until then been the limit of the Yatestoop Sough, towards Gratton, where it was hoped by following the Coast Rake, to cut undiscovered veins beneath the shales. By December 1920 however, with no further capital forthcoming, the adventure was wound up. It was always unrealistic, but for a short time for some it gave real support, and no doubt, hope. Winster especially was undoubtedly split in its loyalties, and it was a both bitter and sad period for the large mining community there. Even today this has been reflected in some of the comments by old miners. The new owners however inherited a union-free mine, with men who had only recently received a large loyalty bonus, and who had a firm understanding of the precariousness of their position.

The Bradford Vale Mining Company and Millclose Mines Ltd

THIS COMPANY was already, for a few months, the owners of Mawstone Mine, near Youlgreave, on the other side of Stanton Moor, where it was hoped, by several generations of owners to find "another Millclose". In February 1919, the mine was put up for sale by tender, including all the surface and underground works. The Lea Lead Works lease was available to the buyer without payment of a premium. Bradford Vale bought Millclose in late 1919, probably for around £120-130,000. The principal operator in this deal was F.H. Chambers the proprietor of the Stanton Ironworks (near Ilkeston), and by mid-March 1920, after he had acquired or renegotiated a series of leases with local landowners, he had sold his holding to a new company, Millclose Mines Ltd, for £160,000, (a higher sum originally agreed was later reduced) of which £103,000 was in cash, the rest in fully paid up £10 shares. The mine was then recapitalised at a value of £275,000, a figure which was later reduced to attract shareholders.

The new company was privately floated, with Chambers, George H. Key, John Green, and Tom Wright (the coal supplier) as major shareholders and directors. It was suggested that some of the deputies in the mine acquired shares, and others were sold privately to friends. These continued to operate the mine until 1922, though with losses rather than profits, partly since the Jumbo engine-house caught fire in 1921, requiring extensive rebuilding under the then engineer A. Richards. In 1922 the capital was reformed and Consolidated Goldfields took a major

27. Lea Lead Works in the 1920s. The large square block, left rear, is a condenser stack for the fumes from the furnaces. It and the chimneys are strapped with iron bands - probably since the mortar is eaten away by the sulphurous fumes. Note the horse and cart - a full load of lead ore would be about six inches deep. (John Henry Marsden Collection).

interest, probably buying Chambers' shares, following a report they commissioned from an eminent consulting mining geologist Dr. Malcolm McLaren. He produced two reports, in 1920 and 1923, both of which are unfortunately missing, though some details are known. McLaren, after discussing the main features of the mine and its geology, considered it probably almost exhausted, but with sufficient potential ore left to enable it to at least partially pay its way, and to allow a full exploration over several years. He warned it was no more than a speculation, but a promising one, and recommended purchase of a substantial shareholding. Subsequently Goldfields provided technical assistance, but though the registered office was at Moorgate in London (the Goldfields Office) and their Robert Annan was Chairman of Directors, Millclose Mines was run locally under Managing Director G.H. Key, with shareholder meetings held either at Matlock's Chatsworth Hydro, or the New Bath Hotel.

Under Goldfields' expertise, there was a large injection of capital into the mine, which allowed both the technical equipment to be overhauled and up-dated, and a proper system of exploration to be undertaken, with the object of always having ore in reserve, rather than the previous hand-to-mouth existence. With the success of this effort, and the large size (by British standards) of the mine, it attracted a great deal of attention in the press and in journals. Together with the memories - some written at the time by professional mining engineers and students - and others of local men who worked at the mine, it is possible for us to have a very full picture of what went on in the twenty years up to 1940. This was to be Millclose's golden age.

Rich prospects ahead

Millclose in the 1920s

IN 1923, THE late Francis Glossop, then a mining student at University, produced a report on the mine as part of his studies, soon after the new company had begun the modernisation. Under Wass and Co. the mine had produced about 160,000 tons of lead ore, and about 7300 tons of zinc blende, by what the young Glossop considered "somewhat primitive methods", whilst in 1923 the mine for the first time had "ore in sight" as the result of recent development and exploratory work. The ore found until then, with the exception of some in the shales, had come from the (top bed of) limestone under the shales, and, he reported the contemporary view, there was little chance of finding ore below the toadstone which lay under the top limestone. He reported that under the new management, modern drilling had been introduced, using mainly Ingersoll drills, rather than the British Holman, and with Gelatine Dynamite. Both had of course been used previously, but hand drilling and black powder had remained in use except on the main drives: now it was to be systematic throughout the mine. They also seem to have introduced drills which used water to suppress dust - the water was taken in in small barrels, though piped water was to follow. An unexpected change found necessary was for drillers to use carbide (acetylene) lamps rather than candles, as the tallow, if it got into the water barrel, clogged the hole in the drill steel. In a number of diagrams, it is made clear how mining was carried out, including the use of gantries or bridges to cross the cavities they found. In the upper levels hand haulage was still necessary, but on the main 73 fathom level (some writers like Glossop already referred to this as the 70 fathom, and most did thereafter), an electric battery locomotive was in use, made by British Electric Vehicles Ltd, with batteries by the Bakewell D.P. Battery Company. As yet the mill was largely unchanged, and the pumping arrangements still mainly depended on the three steam engines, by then working close to their maximum capacity, with a steam pressure of 80 pounds per square inch - three times higher than when they were built a half-century earlier. The aerial ropeway was still in use - though it was taken down a few years later - its doom was probably heralded by the two steam lorries - one by Foden, the other a Robey. Francis Glossop was most

28. General view of the dressing plant in 1923, with the stone breaker on the left, trommels in the centre, jig-house to the right, and a discarded boiler in the foreground. The elevator raised waste to dump into tubs which ran on a bridge-railway to the dump. (Francis Glossop -1923 Report).

29. The Jigging House, probably 1920s. High speed jigs for separating ore. Above the boxes are the line shafts and eccentrics, which killed young Ferdinand White in 1934. (Stone Collection).

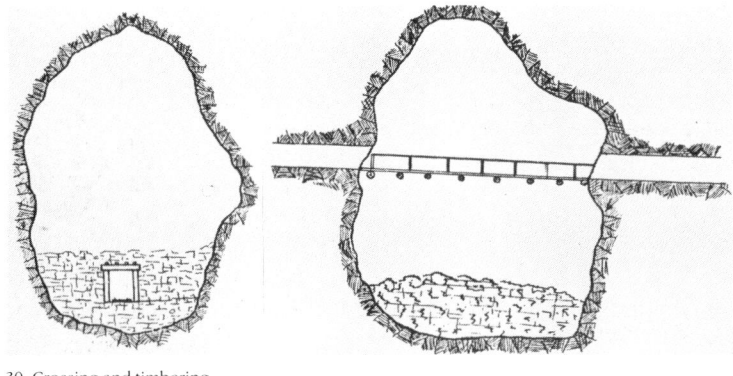

30. Crossing and timbering in cavities. Much of the mine waste from driving in rock was dumped into such cavities. (Glossop - 1923 Report).

impressed by the improved surveying methods. This previously had been carried out solely, when done at all, by a miners' magnetic dial - now there was a fully equipped drawing office, and the main survey used a theodolite. W.W. Varvill, who directed the surveying of the mine, was also a lecturer in mining at Birmingham University.

The very detailed mine maps produced under Varvill enable us to see with great detail where work was done. Between 1920 and 1929, most effort concentrated on working dozens of minor joints and veins to the west of the main vein, under and beyond the village of Stanton Lees, and on the most northern extent of the main vein, a third of a mile or so north of Stanton Lees. Here was found a considerable amount of ore, and with a large number of workplaces operating, production rose reasonably, with small operating profits after 1925, and a particularly good year with very high output in 1929.

Nevertheless, by 1929, most of these opportunities had been exploited, and the Company had accumulated losses of £31,365, of which £24,269 was for the year up to March 1929: and there was a bank overdraft of nearly £59,000. The difficulty of continuing in these circumstances had been foreseen, and around 1925 the decision was taken to sink a shaft downwards - miners call this a winze - near the northern end of the workings on the 70 fathom level. This was where the ore had been particularly rich, and just as importantly, where a strong flow of water emerged. At Millclose it was always considered wise to follow the water, which often led on to the next ore-rich cavity - so many old Millclose men have told us they suggested this was the most likely place, that it is certain it was general opinion. But miners for their jobs will always not unnaturally vote to carry on. Local newspapers also carried a story of two local headmasters, T.D. Franklin of the Stancliffe Hall Boys School at Darley Dale, and Dr. E.H. Chapman of the Ernest Bailey Grammar School. Both had scientific backgrounds, and had invented some form of geo-physical instrument for prospecting. Such instruments were then in their infancy, and though it is not stated, probably it was used to measure resistivity in the rock, which might reasonably be expected to vary when either cavities or veins were within range. They claimed success for their method, though later articles failed to give them any credit. However it was McLaren who recommended the actual project, and Goldfields who ensured the capital was available.

The decision to sink at the "boil up" involved a great act of faith. It was almost certain that by penetrating the toadstone again, and carrying out exploration from it, that new large feeders of water would be met with, which would require major investment in pumping plant to keep the mine open. The new winze, which was soon to be called No. 1

31. Battery locomotive recharging station on the 70 fathom level. Spare sets of 24 cell batteries were charged from a surface DC dynamo. (Stone Collection)

37

32. Ore-bins in the late 1920s. The lorry is Tom Wright's, local coal agent, and director of Millclose Mines. According to Len Millward, who also owned his own lorry at the time, Wright was "making money in his sleep", with 14 loads of coal in a day, and another 28 stockpiled for the weekend. Wright lived at nearby Warney Lea, and had wide local business interests. He died in February 1930 leaving £146,192. (Stone Collection).

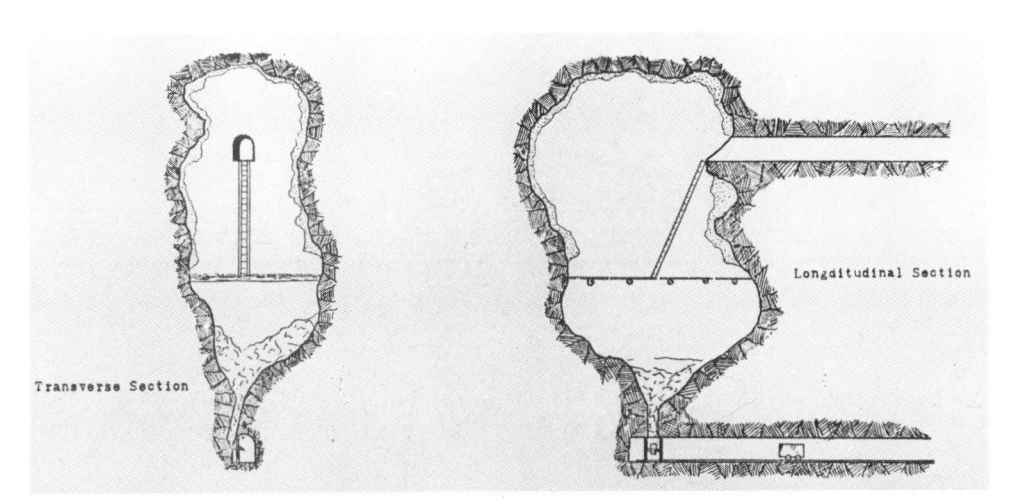

33. The method of working a cavity. A drive was made under the cavity, and a chute fitted, after which ore lining the walls was blasted off. (Glossop Report, 1923)

Winze, was put down from the 70 fathom to 103 fathoms. The toadstone here was surprisingly thin, and soon penetrated, but the flow of water during sinking and subsequent difficulty was very great. Levels were driven off also at 84 and 93 fathoms, and soon found rich ore, which was eventually reached further away on the bottom level; this last was to be the main haulage way, and was about 10 feet wide and 7 feet high. By 1929-30 with rich prospects ahead, a massive investment programme was put in hand.

The first major change was to the pumping system. Jumbo was scrapped, and the engine house partially demolished - the aerial ropeway had gone already, and Frank Toplis who replaced Tom Wright after his death in 1930 was conveying coal and lead ore in motor waggons. More electric pumps were installed underground, and subsequently Baby and Alice only remained on standby. A new diesel engine power-house was put in in case of failure of the local grid, which was now available. Two of the old boilers were used as fuel tanks, though the diesel generator seems to have been rarely used. A new electrically driven Bellis and Morcom compressor was installed, and the old one was converted from steam to electricity. The most conspicuous change visible was a new steel headstock, erected over the Jumbo engine-house and shaft, which had two 500 tons steel bins high above the buildings, one for Haddon, one for Stanton ore. Below, the Jumbo shaft was refitted with pitch-pine guides, for two cages, down to the 70 fathom level. From the bins a chain conveyor and then a rubber conveyor took ore into the adjacent mill. Thereafter Lees Shaft was used only for man-winding, and for equipment. This was all operating by October 1933, and production rose by over 500 tons per week. In the year ending in March 1934, some 81,629 tons of ore had been raised, which dressed to yield 39,757 tons of concentrate. This caused considerable problems at the Lea smelter, and despite installation there of two new Newnham Hearths, some ore had to be sold. Plans were put in hand to erect a new smelter at the mine site, needing only a diesel locomotive to deliver ore from the mill. By the next annual meeting, this was complete, with six Newnham Hearths, and a blast furnace for resmelting the slags. Lea remained at work for the next year, and the combined output rose to 12,177 tons, almost double that of the previous year. Below ground developments

34. The "Boil Up", about 1925. This winze, or underground shaft was sunk into the main-up-welling of water on the 70 fathom level. It was known later as the No.1 Winze. It led to the vast 1930s bonanza. Seen here is the winding skip, with the pipework leading to the pumps. (Stone Collection).

39

35. The electric winder being installed underground, c1930, at No.1 Winze. It wound tubs of ore from the 103 fathom level to the 70 fathom. Frank Land of Bonsall is on the left. (Stone Collection).

36. The electricity power-house of c1934, with Crossley Premier 750 HP Diesels capable of producing 450 kw at 3.3 kv on a GEC generator. After closure these were sent to South Africa with Jimmy Trail, but sank with the ship. (Stone Collection).

included the No. 2 Winze to the 144 fathom level, and hoped for major developments there.

The orebody found on the 129 fathom level - the Main Joint as it was called, created much interest: it was contained in the limestone between two volcanic lavas or toadstones, and filled what was clearly a pre-existing cavern system. Solution by circulating water had caused the original cavern to collapse, and spaces between the blocks had been filled with ore, and much of the blocks in turn had been dissolved and replaced with mineral. Miners have described it as a cavern over 1000 feet long, but it seems they probably exaggerated a little, pardonably enough in the small pools of light they worked with. The main cavern was, according to the surveyors, about 400 feet long, 40 feet high, and 60-100 feet wide, after which it divided into two or three. On the west side were also found a series of "wing deposits", infilling joints and cross-joints, sometimes extending a thousand feet and more. At this depth a new factor was the presence of considerable zinc blende, enough to make recovery profitable, and this is probably a major factor in the decision to introduce a flotation process to the dressing plant, replacing, in 1936, the use of tables for fine ore. Flotation required much more finely ground material, which required the use of ball mills in the circuit. It was undoubtedly the most modern, and greatest lead mine that the country had ever known.

37. The Warrencarr Shaft Headgear, during construction in 1933. The two large ore-bins, one for each royalty, were made by Plowright Brothers of Chesterfield. Note the reduced "Jumbo" engine house. "Seven years later they came down again". (Stone Collection).

38. Warrencarr Hoist in 1936 - 80 HP with a 440v induction motor. Harry Moore was one of the winding-men. He used spare time, including whilst the hoist was in motion, to carry out his hobby of painting on the rear wall. He lost this job after the cage was overwound into the catch-hooks. (Stone Collection).

39. A new set of jigs being installed about 1930. (John Henry Marsden Collection).

40. The diesel Loco - a 3 1/2 ton "Planet" by Hibberd and Co, with a two cylinder 20 HP Blackstone engine, in 1936. It moved concentrate from the bins to the new smelter, and tailings waste to the dump about a quarter mile away. Drivers were John Percy Marsden and Jock Boden. (Stone Collection).

42

43

41. The blast furnace for treating slags in the new smelter, in 1936. Note the ingots piled in front. (Stone Collection).

42. Air cooled flues for the fumes from the smelter - they then passed through a "bag-house" to trap dust, and then through lime-water sprays to remove sulphur dioxide. (Stone Collection).

43. A Hardinge Ball Mill (it used cast iron balls) for grinding ore down to a degree sufficient for the flotation process. There is a Newall Mill in the background. "You couldn't get away with it empty, the foreman (Sam or Fred Stone) could hear the balls rattling inside". (British Speleological Association Collection, BCRA.).

44. Flotation tanks - the ore in a slurry or "pulp" is agitated to form bubbles with a tar oil (similar to disinfectant), to which particles of lead ore, or zinc ore will attach themselves. The bubbles overflow into a launder, and are "killed" with sprays of water, seen right. By adjusting the chemistry, different materials can be separated in turn - it is still one of the most important processes in the modern world. (Stone Collection).

The mine that drowned

Millclose's Last Few Years

IN 1936 HOWEVER a new, or more properly, an old problem again occurred. In February huge new quantities of water entered the mine. Whereas in 1932 an average of 2350 gallons had to be raised per minute, in 1937, this had risen to 4300. The 1936 flood caused most of the miners to be laid off for several weeks, whilst the engineers struggled to cope with the inrush, which came from the Pilhough Fault, and there were fears and strong rumours the mine would close. This was cleared, but a further and even greater flood took place on the 25th of February 1938, when a shot, drilled by Fred Boam of Winster, blasted into the Pilhough Fault, at the then northernmost part of the mine, on the 144 fathom level. It might have been even worse had new pumps not been recently installed, but even so it flooded all the mine up to the 103 fathom level before it could be checked. Fortunately all the miners escaped unhurt in the rush to the surface, though it was a close run thing. Again some 400 miners were laid off, and new pumps had to be ordered and installed, and again, after ten weeks, the mine was pumped dry, but with the flow per minute permanently increased by over 1000 gallons; in all some 5550 gallons per minute, nearly 8 million gallons per day, or in weight, almost 36,000 tons a day, much of it eventually from nearly a thousand feet depth. It was an enormous financial burden for the mine.

45. A group photograph taken after the installation of the new pumps in 1938. Left to right: Walter Boam, Ernest Moseley, Peter Marshall, John Henry Smith, Bill Marshall, Stan Else, Dick Slack. (Ron Slack Collection).

46. The source of the 1938 flood on the 144 fathom level near Pilhough Fault - still delivering some 3000 gallons per minute, even after it was successfully pumped. (Mrs Joy Lomas - nee Rhode, collection).

47. Plan and section of the Millclose Mine as it was after development work ceased in June 1940. The final "Stinkwater Raise" at the north end explored the ground under the shale, below Stanton Hall, without any successful find.

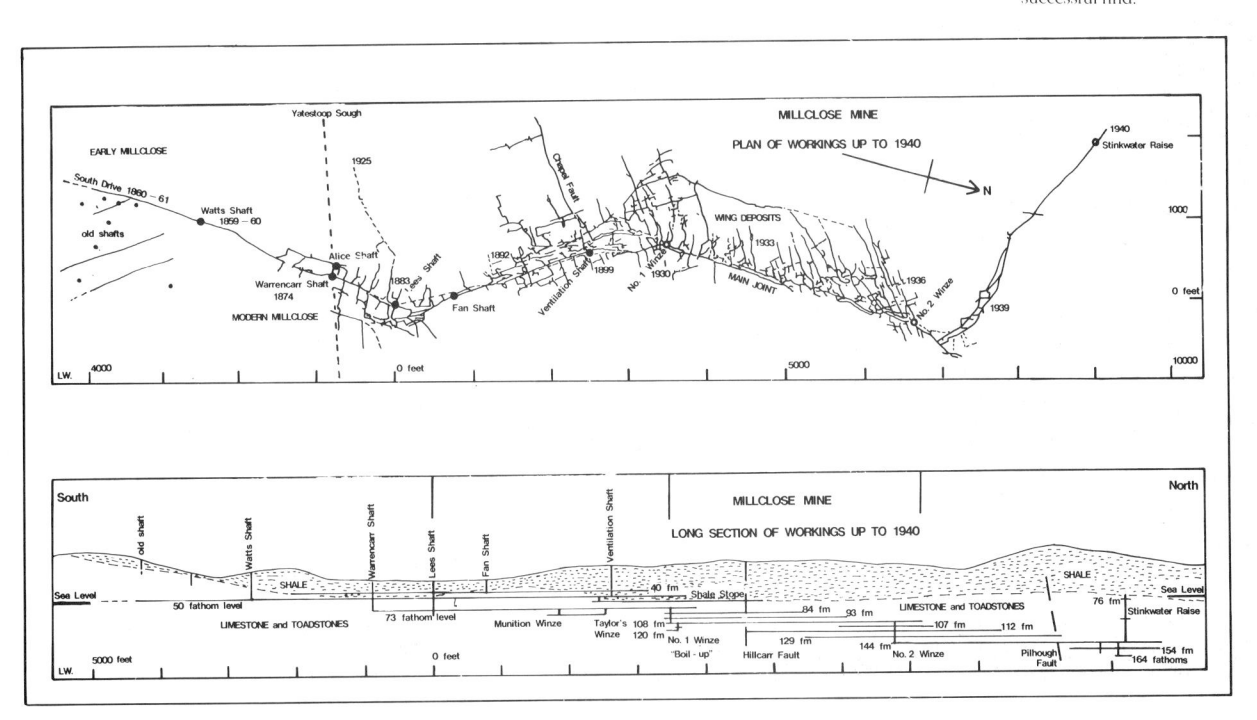

Nevertheless, the results for 1937-38 were again good, and but for the flood would have been higher than for the previous year. Some 104,610 tons were raised, yielding 13,521 tons of lead concentrate, and 16,543 tons of zinc, though some 6000 tons of the latter were from low grade concentrates kept from the year before. Unfortunately there had been delays, due to Government action, in the supplies of steel, and the new flotation plant had been only in partial production for a time, and subsequently there had been a great fall in the price of metals.

Despite optimism about the probable discovery of further ore reserves in the annual report for 1937-38, all was not well, and the promising indications were not to be borne out. From the 144 fathom level, developments - tunnels, raises, and winzes - thoroughly explored the mine. At the furthermost end, a raise was put upwards, searching for indications of the vein above for a total height of some 400 feet, to no avail. Winzes were put down to 154 fathoms, and 164 fathom levels, but again the ground was barren. In May 1939 proposals were put to shareholders to increase capital in the mine to enable development work finally to seek the massive quantities of ore required to stay viable. The main impetus came from the manager, Leslie B. Williams, who persuaded the directors that shareholders would wish a last effort to keep the mine open. By June 1939 there were well founded rumours that the mine was to close. The efforts of the recent months had proved unsuccessful, and it is clear the directors had made the decision to clear out the mine's remaining reserves, and then cease operations. In June 1940, mining operations finally ceased, and thereafter the surface plant was used only for retreatment of residues of zinc in the surface tips, even this due to finish by the end of the year. The mine itself finally closed, after six weeks of salvage operations, in August 1940. The smelter however remained in use until the end of February 1941, when the plant was sold in going order to the present owners, Messrs H.J. Enthoven and Sons Ltd. The greater part of the mine plant was quickly sold - the war provided both a ready market for scrap, and for secondhand up-to-date equipment, and the prices gained were regarded as "very satisfactory". The treatment plant however remained in use through the war, supported by the Ministry of Supply, but in 1945 was sold to William Twigg, steel merchants at Matlock.

There have been endless post-mortems about Millclose. Many miners, and some management considered that greater efforts should have been made. A. McCall, who had been one of the surveyors, felt that the mine closed simply because the stoping - the actual extraction of ore, had been allowed to run ahead of exploration. W.W. Varvill the surveyor, who wrote substantially on the mine then and since, felt that the main reason was that the cost of pumping was so high as to make further work unprofitable. Others considered it had indeed been fully explored, and there was not sufficient ore to work it properly. Certainly enormous effort was put into the final exploration, and only a magnificent find (wartime subsidised working excepted) could have allowed it to stay open for more than a few months.

Five candles a shift

Old Miners Recollect the 1920s and 1930s

A LARGE MINE, as Millclose was this century, has a great variety of jobs as well as the actual mining. In the 1930s for when we have the additional benefit of living memories to help us, the work of the mine was divided into departments:- the office with its clerical work and of course the weekly pay (Bill Bateman's job); the mechanical and engineering departments which looked after the enormous amount of equipment; the dressing plant which treated the run-of-the-mine ore and turned it into a saleable concentrate; and the surveyors and geologist. The smelter always seemed to be treated separately, even after it came to the mine, though it too was a department.

The overall responsibility was that of the Managing Director, George H. Key, and under him, the General Manager, Leslie B. Williams. Williams and his underground manager, Jack Rhodes, were both Australian (the latter of German extraction), no doubt appointed by Goldfields. Underground, the mine was worked over three shifts of eight hours; day, afternoon, and nightshifts. Each shift had a shift boss or deputy - Harold Wild, shown in one of the photographs was a deputy along with Ted Gladwin, others were Jack Staton and Goff Taylor, and Joe Needham and Jack Gregory, and there was also a foreman or deputy foreman: this was much more supervision than had been traditional. The miners were fairly specialised, though if capable expected to do one another's jobs if necessary - developers (drilling and blasting), end-men (face-workers) and fillers (of ore into tubs), timbermen, waggoners or haulage men. There were also the "powder monkeys" - Walter Gratton and his mate Tommy Austin, whose jobs were to keep the locked wooden boxes underground full of gelignite, fuses and detonators. Miners brought out their own worn drills for re-sharpening by the blacksmith, George Thomas, near the top of Lees Shaft, and collected them again on a later shift. Care was taken to keep them labelled, as someone was always ready to use someone

48. The suspension bridge over the Derwent, possibly 1912, with probably Daniel Morgan on it. It gave access to the aerial ropeway, but at first was strictly otherwise a management "perk", controlled by a lock on the gate, for those who lived in Darley Dale. It was demolished in the 1960s. (Morgan Collection).

49. The picking table and jig operators in 1932. Top - Harry Bowmer of Holloway, Fred Flint of Wensley, Wilf Spencer of Bonsall, Dick Bond of Winster, Edward Stevenson of Rowsley. Middle - Stan Marshall of Winster, Owen Smith of Bonsall, George Kenworthy (of no fixed abode), Stanley Maynes of Cross Green, Charlie Stewartson of Matlock. Bottom - Eric Fisher of Winster, Harry Goodwin of Birchover, and Harold Boam of Winster. (Eric Fisher Collection).

else's sharpened drills.

Only a few jobs required men to be technically qualified - and most of these were part of the senior management of the mine, often brought in from outside the area. Earlier this had largely been from Cornwall, and such men as Daniel Morgan received special privileges - being allowed to use the "swing", or suspension bridge across the river for example, though later it was used by anyone from the Darley side. By the 1920s mining was an international industry, and indeed when the mine closed more than a few left for mining overseas, notably to South Africa. Other jobs were traditional crafts, like that of George Thomas, the blacksmith (son of Captain Stephen Thomas mentioned earlier), who when offered a job by Ingersolls because of his ability at drill sharpening, received extra wages, or of Jesse Wild the joiner, remembered for his trick of engaging people in conversation whilst he nailed their jackets to a piece of wood. Some others came to the mine as students, to gain experience, usually recommended by W.W. Varvill the surveyor. Most however learnt their skills on-the-job, though it was not always easy to match the old-time skills to the rapid changes which took place at Millclose, and men from Winster, who looked on the mine as their own, sometimes seem to have resented newcomers, and their ideas.

Working at Millclose was looked on as a good job, "you were made once you started because there was no lost time like the other industries of farming and quarrying". Eric Fisher of Winster began as a lad of fourteen just out of school, in 1930 on the picking table

50. Eric Fisher in 1940, assistant surveyor, carrying a carbide (acetylene) lamp. Note the safety helmet, worn by men in the later photographs only. It is the Lees Shaft, with the curved roof of the Blacksmith's shop behind. (Eric Fisher Collection).

51. On the way to work, at Lees Shaft in 1936 - a favourite place for such photographs. Several are wearing thigh boots - usually for pumpmen only, and given the date, it is probably the crew putting in new pumps after the flood. Note the safety lamps - the flood may have disrupted the ventilation system. (Left to right) - E. Needham of Darley, Mick Hardy (the banksman) of Wensley, Arthur Marshall of Winster, Frank Land of Bonsall, Percy Boam of Winster, Jim Wood of Wensley, Bill Mosley of Wensley, Cecil Newton of Winster, Wilf Stevenson of Stanton Lees, Joe Vardy of Darley. (Eric Fisher Collection).

at 3s-6d a day. After a number of little jobs, he became assistant to the surveyor (Varvill), which had the advantage of getting him to most parts of the mine, and let him get an idea of the geology. Many miners saw little outside their own area, in which they could work for years. John Marsden, another lad at the picking table, moved on to the blacksmith's shop, at 5s-0d a day, to replace the blacksmith's mate who had gone underground for 8s-2d. Horace Woodhouse of Darley Bridge was already married when he started in 1929 - his father-in-law got him his job ahead of many others, and he went below that same night at 10 pm with no previous underground experience, "working with an real old-time miner called Jonathon Roose from Elton". In time he went on to tramming tubs to the haulage level, then a variety of jobs to teach him the basic mining skills of timbering, rail-laying, drilling, blasting etc, after which he became a development man and shaftsman. At weekends, when the mine was short of a deputy, he, on development work, became deputy for the day. He was one of the last to work at the mine in 1940, stripping out the shaft. Such skilled men on drilling and blasting of headings could earn up to 16s-0d a shift, plus bonus, though about 10 shillings was more usual. Work at surface was no less hard, but generally paid less. Men were generally first put to stoking the boilers, a non-stop job. Flames often shot out of the firebox and burnt the men when the wind blew down the chimney if they failed to duck in time. "They were given a good job after a few months on the boilers"!

Lees Shaft was used to wind men down to their work, and they had to be there at starting time already changed in the stripping coe, and with their lamps or five candles, and of course, any tea and food, which they called their "snap". Generally they wore a shirt and thick, hard-wearing moleskin trousers, and clogs, though some tried wellingtons, but these were easily ripped by the rock. Pumpmen had thigh-boots, and when these wore out, miners used the long tops as additional leg-protection against water. In wet places they also wore oilskins and helmets. The winder at Lees Shaft was still steam powered, "one of the most primitive devices I have ever seen". It was started by the hoist-man kicking a hook out of an eye, and engaging it with a lever, after which it was worked up to full speed using the steam. Near the end of the run the driver again kicked the hook to catch the lever, and by working the steam against the piston, brought it to a halt. Other shafts had electric winders, but, as one old miner said sarcastically, "this one was only for men". "It was certainly of historical interest". At one time the engineman acted as the boilerman as well, and it is related that one of them was wont to leave the lever after starting, go to light his pipe at the boiler, then dash back to stop the engine. Herbert Hardy, engineman, was renowned for knocking the engine out of gear to drop the cage, arresting its downward progress just before the bottom. Nevertheless, though a few waggons were dragged over the sheaves, there was never a man-winding accident.

Once at levels, either 50 fathom or 70 fathom, the miners walked to work - riding on locomotives was forbidden, though a ride in a tub was sometimes possible, avoiding the walking through ankle or knee high water. It could be as much as two miles to the workplace, taking up to an hour, with, to get to the end of the mine, two or more winzes to climb down, and then further along, possibly several hundred feet to climb up, and all again to come out.

The best and fittest miners went on to development work, working with a mate to do the mucking out. This meant driving a tunnel for exploration, or raises (up-shafts) or winzes to open out an ore body. They usually used Ingersoll drills for horizontal or up-holes, and the very heavy Holman jack-hammers for down. On main levels a column and bar mounted drill was used - which weighed some 250 pounds. Once holes were drilled, they were charged with dynamite, and the safety fuse was lit: the holes were so drilled, and the lengths of fuses designed, that first a wedge of ore was driven out from the centre, after which side holes blew with maximum effect into the cavity left. It was skilled, and potentially dangerous work. An air hose was left open in the heading for half an hour to clear the fumes, whilst the driller and his mate had "snap" and hot tea from bottles or cans heated over candle stumps. After this came mucking out into the tubs for the hauliers to take away to the haulage level. In stopes, such as the wing deposits, the end men drilled so as to bring the ore down, either into a chute, to be fed under gravity to tubs in the haulage level, or to the ground for hand shoveling. In many cases the work was done precariously standing high in the roof on a single plank. In some "end-places", it was not profitable to bring a level under the deposit, so that the "clean-up men" had to haul ore up using hand operated windlasses. Often this job was in charge of an older experienced miner, who would search out any possible leaders which might go on to more ore.

In some areas the work was extremely simple, such as the large cavities on the 129 fathom level. Here the main work was to break the ore up, by picks or using "John Nobel", and shovel it into tubs. It could however be dangerous work, under the toadstone roof, and "pig-sties" of cross-timbers, filled with waste rock were built up to support the roof. Heavy timbers squeezed to thin under the pressure. It was here that Harry Mayall was killed instantly in 1939 by a fall of a long

52. Everard Waterfall (right) with his blue enamelled tea-can, and George Bowmer of Bonsall. The gate on the shaft behind them lifted as the cage arrived. (Miss Monica Waterfall Collection).

53

section of roof, and his mate Vic Littlewood had a leg broken. Others may also have been injured - Thomas Smallwood has been mentioned. Harry was carried out in sacks on two planks, and Vic after he recovered was given light work at the surface.

There were other dangers too. Though the mine was gassy and placed by the Mines' Inspector therefore under the "special regulations", there was a notably free and easy attitude to smoking. This was perhaps since though safety lamps had to be carried to pass through the upper parts of the mine near the shales, in the lower parts candles and acetylene lamps were used, and ordinary safety fuse was lit with matches for blasting.

Several accounts remark on the men smoking when deputies were not present, and vice versa. Breaking the law in this way demanded at least some common sense of course. A cautionary tale still told is of Charlie Shimwell who smoked in the upper gassy part of the mine. He was badly burnt and had his ears blown off. Another gas which caused problems was hydrogen sulphide, the "rotten eggs" gas. It dissolves in water, which gave developers such as Horace Taylor at the far end of the mine in the late 30s a very tough time, giving them "red-eye" and sometimes temporarily blinding them. The area where this was found was known as "Stinkwater Raise".

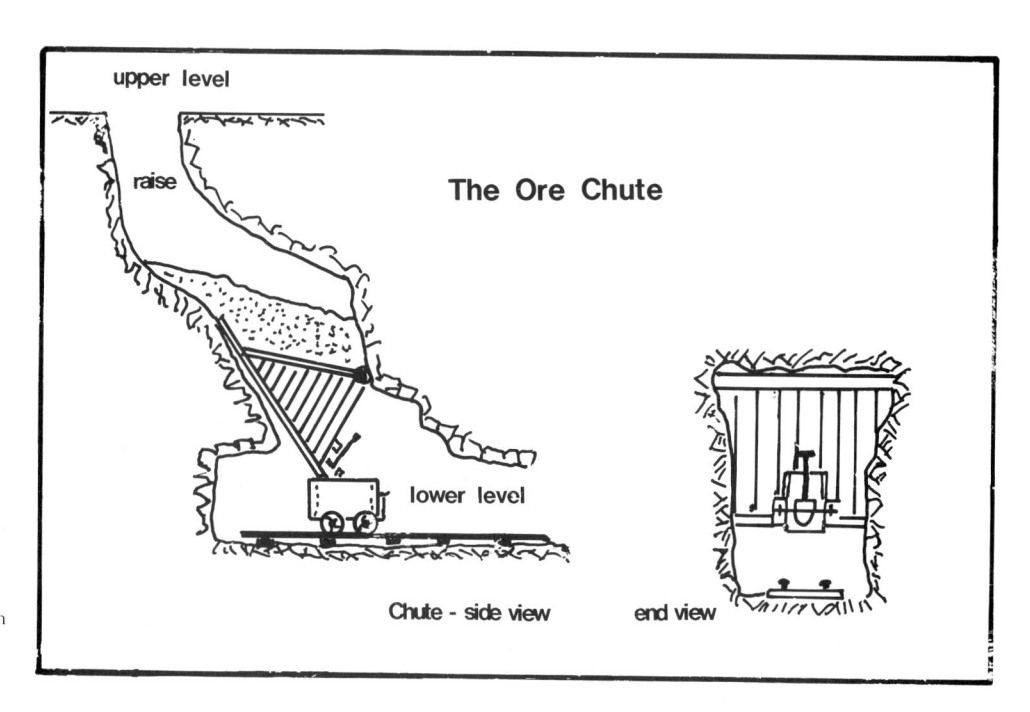

53. Sketches by J. Foster Smith of methods used in stoping - late 1930s, in a typical "wing-deposit. (PDMHS. Bulletin).

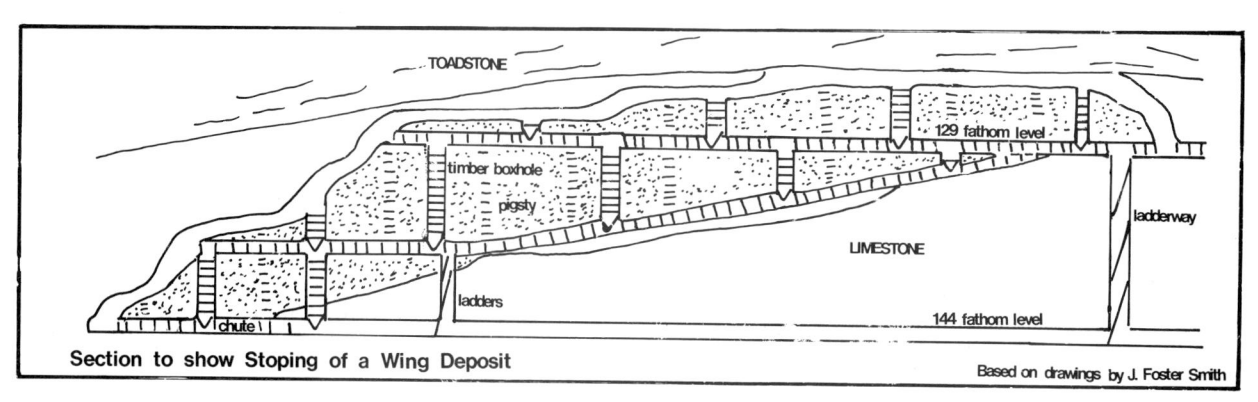

"Millclose was a terribly wet place". Developers especially had a tough job. For instance when they deliberately sank into the "boil-up". Water under high pressure often incessantly sprayed into the workings at drive ends, "so strong it pushed away loaded wagons", even forcing them to use electric battery lamps. Working often had to be done at the face by the machine (drilling) men under a canvas for protection. In the great flood of 1938 water under high pressure poured through a hole two feet or more across. The huge flow streamed down the level towards the ladders and safety. Because "levels" in fact slope towards the outlet, this meant the men at the far end were in grave danger of being trapped.

Frank Green was one of those working at the end of the 144 level: "We had drilled and charged the holes, and with the fuses lit, retired back and up the raise for safety. If you didn't get clear, you were liable to be hit with flying debris. You could tell when it was a good round, but the shots went off with a peculiar noise, and it wasn't a good round at all. Then there was a rush of air, and the rest of the round went off. Something was very wrong. When we climbed down to the level we were nearly swept off our feet by water. I had an acetylene lamp which I dropped. Everyone was making their way to the shaft, and one of my mates called to me to leave it, and get out, and I didn't need telling twice. Fortunately the cage was waiting for us when we reached the shaft. It was a blessing no one was on the 120 at the time". One of those pulled from the water on to the ladders as he struggled to safety was Bernard Hearn, the foreman electrician, who was covered from head-to-foot in yellow slime, which also caused the river to run yellow for a few days. Suitably, it was the pump-men who were last out.

Amongst the most skilled and toughest jobs were those in shafts. It might be sinking them, or equipping them with timber for compartments and cage guides. The main winding shaft, replacing the Jumbo pumps,

54. Drilling on the 93 fathom level, ready for blasting - cleaning up ore. Walter Boam (right) and Cyril Land. (Foster Smith Collection).

55

55. Winding stowes at the top of a clean-up winze down to the bottom of a wing deposit, on the 93 fathom level, with left, Frank Staton. (Foster Smith collection).

was timbered by George Shimwell, using four plumb bobs suspended for accuracy: during the work another Winster man fell but survived - he never came back! During the removal of cables from this shaft, just before the mine finally closed, Horace Taylor had a narrow escape, when the cable, attached to the bottom of the cage, failed to come free. There was a bang, and the strain stretched open the chain links holding the cage. Had they entirely parted, it would have crashed to the bottom since there was no form of safety catch.

At the surface the ore went to the dressing plant, which was always fairly advanced, but in the late 1930s, very modern indeed. Even so there was still plenty of hand work, and the labour of young lads out of school was still cheap enough for their use on the picking belt - another job calculated to make most other things enjoyable. With the adoption of ball mills for grinding for flotation, a great deal of old waste was re-treated - for which a tunnel was driven under the gravel or waste-heap, a "nice piece of mining", so as to draw off the material using a gravel pump. The gravel was washed into the pump by jets of water from monitors. In charge of the plant was a manager and chemist called Meritt. He was unpopular and one day his car was once part covered in gravel tipped from the bridge over which waste gravel passed to the dump. On another occasion he sacked two men who left a derailed waggon for the next shift. It is suspected they were the same men. Daft things were done also, like Joe Webster who for a bet rode the "flight" or aerial ropeway across the river to Darley. Amongst those who worked in the dressing plant was Sam Stone of Winster who was a shift foreman. A substantial part of his photographic collection appears in this book.

Accidents of any severity were usually more rare at surface than underground, but in 1934 young Ferdinand White of Darley Dale, aged 18, arrived on shift to work on the jigs (see

56. Another group at Lees in 1936. Not all are known, but, left to right, standing; ?, Jack Taylor of Wensley, Joseph Spencer of Hackney, ?, ?, ?, ?, Frank Coleman of Darley, ?, George Greatorex of Wensley, ?, ?, ?, ?, ?, ?, ?, ?, Joseph Webster of Wensley, Vernon Wild of Wensley, G. Bowen of Darley. Seated; George Harrison of Darley, Frank Glossop of Elton, ?, Albert Webb, Harry Mayall of Darley - who was killed on the 129 level in 1939, and Jim Wood of Wensley. (Eric Fisher Collection).

57. Millclose Mine Football Team in 1938. Left to right, rear: Mr. Mitchell (surface manager), Alan Dakin (not at Millclose), Herbert Webster, Lew Barker, Vic Dakin, Don Taylor, Edmund Shimwell, Arnie Shimwell, Charlie Shimwell, Jack Phillips, Jim Bark (I/C developers). Front: Maurice Wild, Harry Evans, Frank Bates, Bill Bates, Cliff Webster, Arnie Webster, Bert Webster, Wilf Dakin (not a Millclose man). (Frank Bates Collection).

photograph 29) a few minutes late at 6.03 am. Four minutes later he was dead, his scarf tangled in the eccentrics as he was oiling it. On the 10th of May 1938, an even worse accident occurred, during loading of an old waste heap for retreatment in the dressing plant. Four men were at work, loading a lorry, when the heap collapsed, probably as they had hit a soft patch of fine material, immediately burying one, and then as they went to his aid, the other three as well. Rescuers rushed to the tip, finding James Byatt, an older man and ex-coal-miner alive, though badly injured, but found two of the men dead, Thomas Ball of Elton, and Victor Barnes of Ashford, and three hours later found another, Richard Bond of Bonsall. They were all aged about twenty.

On a lighter note, Millclose also had its social side - such as, in Wass' time, the annual excursion for employees by train. Another, and perhaps then the most important, was its football team - "you were made if you could play football". In 1938 the team won the fiercely fought Cavendish Cup. Alas, its fortunes, like those of the mine, deteriorated in 1939. That year saw the break-up of the work-force. Luckily, if you had been a Millclose miner, "you could get a job in a mine anywhere", and many did. One, at the news of closure, cycled quickly to the Matlock Dole Office, informed them of 300 men becoming redundant, and got himself a job relieving his erstwhile workmates. Jimmy Trail, one of the geologists, is said to have declared he was "leaving a sinking ship": he was unfortunate enough to join another, on the way to Africa. Others of course joined one or other of the forces, a few never to return.

Conclusions

Three Centuries of Mining

IN ITS THREE hundred years life, Millclose provided some 450,000 tons of lead and zinc concentrates, more than any other single Derbyshire mine, and perhaps a fifth or a quarter of all the ore ever mined in the County. For many years in its last 80 years of life, it provided a third of British production. It helped also to maintain a local lead industry until just before the war, notably Cox and Co., of Derby, producing mainly white lead for paint. It has also left behind one of the major lead smelters in the UK, still owned by H.J. Enthoven and Sons, who remain an important local employer.

All mines have to close sometime, and inevitably, it is a sad occasion when a mine as prolific and long lasting as Millclose came to its end, despite the tragedies also associated with it. Few other local lead mines worked long enough to have three and even four generations working in them, one after the other, and Millclose was a very "family mine", despite its size. In its time it provided a large

58. The legacy - the front of a Newnam Hearth - with mechanical rabble, for smelting lead in the Enthoven owned works in March 1950. (H.J. Enthoven Collection).

number of families with their living, and spanned the transition from traditional mining, for which Derbyshire was famous, into the modern age, in which Derbyshire is little more than a footnote in the mining books. Despite its large output, the costs also were very high, and it is unlikely any real profit was made after all expenses were accounted for in the last two decades of its life. For local people, it provided in this "golden age", a bridge through the worst trade slump ever experienced. It provided, if not prosperity, a reasonable living, not just for mine employees, but for all the others who depended on it and them for a living. Millclose and its miners deserve to be remembered.

59. A spectacular layout of ingot or pig-moulds during pouring, in front of two 60 ton refining pots, June 1951. (H.J. Enthoven Collection).

Glossary

Soke and Wapentake of Wirksworth

This is the ancient division of Derbyshire, dating from before the Norman Conquest, which for lead mining purposes is still retained. The Soke and Wapentake is divided into mining liberties, roughly the same as present parishes - such as Wensley. The other main lead mining area is the High Peak, which includes the nearby Liberty of Winster: regulations are similar but not identical in the two areas. The lead rights in what are known as customary liberties are owned by the Duchy of Lancaster, the Queen.

At Wirksworth is the Barmoot Hall, where twice annually near Michaelmas and Ladyday, the Duchy's Steward, Barmaster (Bergmeister - the mountain master, a word perhaps over a thousand years old derived from Saxony), and Jury of twelve miners meet to settle any business concerning lead mining. Many old customs remain, including the paying of a "freeing dish" of the first ore got out of a vein, for each meer - a length along the vein, in the Soke and Wapentake, of 29 yards. The record of payment of the freeing dish is the title to the vein. A bronze dish is still kept in the Barmoot Hall, by which the wooden working dishes are calibrated.

Payment of a freeing dish thus indicated the then position of mining, though abuse was not infrequent.

Lot is the duty paid on subsequent ore mined, originally every thirteenth dish. Other duties or royalties include cope - 6d for each load of nine dishes of ore, and though not paid in all liberties, tithe - the tenth dish, was paid originally to the church, but after the Dissolution of the Monasteries in the 16th century, usually to lay "improprietors". Duty ore had to have been made merchantable, that is ready for sale, and was later known as concentrate.

At Millclose, the large amount of ore led to weighing rather than the traditional measuring, and most duties had in practice been reduced from these earlier levels by the late 19th century. These rules only applied to the customary liberties. The liberties of Haddon and Stanton, where most Millclose ore was mined this century were private, that is, not affected by the lead mining customs, and royalties etc. had to be negotiated with the landowner as for any other mineral.

Lead ore

The main ore of lead found in Derbyshire is galena (lead sulphide). It is also found as an oxidised ore, either cerussite and anglesite (lead carbonate and sulphate), but these are comparatively unimportant. It is found in association with zinc ore - blende or sphalerite (zinc sulphide), with at Millclose, the latter increasing in proportion at depth. These ores, and other minerals, such as pyrite (iron sulphide), and especially calcite (calcium carbonate), fluorite or fluorspar (calcium fluoride), and barite (barium sulphate) are found in veins. The minerals have been deposited from warm salty water, squeezed out of deep-buried sediments to the east, flowing to outlets on the surface some 180-275 millions of years ago. The minerals filled cavities formed by faults, or cracks and joints in the limestone rock, many of which were opened out into caverns by earlier water, or the mineralised water itself flowing through. Often the ore was richest at intersections of joints, so that the tapering off over distance led to a wing-like excavation, leading to the use of the term "wing deposit".

Some of the largest deposits were in pipes or flats - long and narrow tube-like deposits or thin and wide respectively, found again mainly in the limestone just under impervious rocks such as the shales and toadstones (volcanic lavas). The mineralising fluids seem to have risen as they flowed, leaving deposits in a stepped zone determined by faults or weaknesses in the otherwise impervious toadstones. Deposition was probably caused as the upflowing water reacted with groundwater - which would cause the amount of ore to decline at depth.

Working the ore

Mining has its own specialised words, and since miners came from different areas, they often brought their own words with them. The top of the shaft was known as the day, and just inside, as the collar. Around the top were buildings for the blacksmith, or for changing - known locally as coes - smithy-coe, stripping-coe, respectively.

If a pumping engine used the shaft, then it had high shear legs from which pipes and other items could be lowered - whilst the pumps included the pipes which brought water to surface, and were known as a lift, or at an earlier time when made of wood, as a pump-tree.

The man who drove the winding engine was variously called the winding-man, the engineer, the tenter (attender), or the hoistman. He lowered the cage which carried the wheeled tubs, or the skip running in slides to carry ore, or the bucket or kibble if it hung free. Underground, the miners got out a level, the depth of which was usually expressed in fathoms (six feet), as the result of Cornish influence. These were based on depths from a single shaft for the whole mine, so for other shafts were notional. At Millclose, a change in the choice of shafts for the base led to much confusion, and the 70 and 73 fathom level was the same! As well as levels (which are in fact just slightly inclined), the miner uses terms for tunnels such as drifts, which incline up or down, crosscuts, which cut through solid rock between veins, and drives, which follow along or roughly parallel to the vein.

Tunnelling for access to new or existing veins is called development, with the working face traditionally known as the forefield. A shaft sunk to the forefield was often known as the forefield shaft, and supplied air and made removal of ore, water, and waste rock easier. Working the vein for its ore is called stoping - a word which derives from the large steps by which it is excavated, rather as quarries have benches. Underhand stoping works downwards, using a stowes (stoce) to hand-wind up the ore, whilst overhand stoping works upwards, allowing ore to fall under gravity, usually via chutes into tubs or waggons running on rails, which take the ore back to the shaft. Underground shafts are known as winzes - another Cornish word, which replaced the Derbyshire sump, if they are sunk downwards, and raises if they were excavated upwards. Raising and underhand stoping were much more efficient methods, and were used where possible.

Dressing the ore

In Derbyshire this was also known as washing, and until the flotation process was used, depended for its success on the different specific gravities of the minerals. Lead ore has a high specific gravity, it feels "heavy", and zinc ore rather less, whilst the other minerals are much lighter. Because of the cost, it was normal as far as possible to pick out good ore and total waste as early as possible - it was the mixed ore and waste, and the smaller particles which had to be dressed. For gravity separation to work well, the pieces need to be of similar size, so they had to be sized, for large pieces using a rotating riddle called a trommel - simply a drum with holes of a set size in it, rotating on an axle. Smaller pieces were dealt with in a classifier, which depended on an upwardly rising current of water in a cone. When sized the larger pieces were jigged, by pulsing water upwards through the ore placed in a sieve. By inclining the sieve, the waste, which was lifted more than the heavy ore by the water, moved downhill, and eventually poured off as a slurry into a launder - a wood or iron trough - and away to the hillock or waste heaps. Ore was retained at the jig, and was periodically removed. The earlier hutches, used before 1883, used the same principle, but were hand operated, and moved the sieve rather than pulsed the water.

Buddling is the process of treating the slimes by pouring them in a slurry over a gentle slope, so that the lead ore is deposited first, the useless waste last. Early buddles were made of wood or stone, and looked like a shallow trench. Round buddles poured the slime over a central cone, and could thus treat more ore in a single operation. The treated ore, ready for sale, was termed concentrate.

Acknowledgements

This book is an early part of a project to explore more fully the history of Millclose, by members of the Peak District Mines Historical Society, and Peak District Mining Museum at Matlock Bath, Derbyshire. We have contacted a large number now of ex-Millclose Miners, and hope to meet more over the next few years - and we are extremely grateful to them for sharing their experiences, and hope they can call at the Museum to see something of their history, as a thankyou to them. Please contact the Museum if you can help further. We have been very fortunate to receive, or to be able to make copies of, a great many photographs. These are acknowledged separately, but particularly valuable collections were donated by Mrs. Stone of Winster; by the Morgan Family; by Eric Fisher of Winster; Paul Deakin; P.B. Smith; J.R. Foster Smith; and the late Francis Glossop. We are grateful too, to the Derbyshire Record Office, Derbyshire County Library, and to Andrew McBeth, Cash and Co., Wirksworth who have made collections available for publication, and to Mrs. Michael Brooke-Taylor, who gave especial permission to use twentieth century documents on deposit in the Record Office earlier than is normally possible. The heading "Five candles a shift", the title of a book he never wrote, is borrowed with his permission, from Eric Fisher. We have also drawn extensively on accounts of Millclose Mine published in the Bulletin of the Peak District Mines Historical Society, and on material in the Society's own collections, and on information and photographs collected by members. Thanks to all.

Note: The site of Millclose Mine is within the works of H.J. Enthoven and Sons, and the Lees Shaft area within that of the Steetley Company, and access is only possible with the prior permission of those companies. There is a footpath close by the Watts Shaft, from which it can be viewed. Beware of dangerous shafts in the area.

The three authors are all members of Peak District Mines Historical Society which operates the Peak District Mining Museum at Matlock Bath, Derbyshire. Lynn Willies is a lecturer at Chesterfield College of Technology and Arts; Keith Gregory is a Laboratory Manager at H.J. Enthoven and Sons; Harry Parker is a former Picture Editor for Sheffield Newspapers Ltd., and in retirement is still an active professional photographer.

SOME MORE DERBYSHIRE TITLES FROM SCARTHIN BOOKS

Pauper's Venture : Children's Fortune The Lead Mines and Miners of Brassington. Ron Slack. 52pp. ISBN 0907758 18 5 £3.00. A study of the lead-mining community of Brassington. Illustrated. Gazetteer of sites.

The Coal Mines of Buxton Alan Roberts and John Leach. 96pp. ISBN 0 907758 10 £3.75. An absorbing study of the forgotten pits and pitmen of the Buxton area. Photographs, maps and diagrams.

Ancient Wells and Springs of Derbyshire Peter J. Naylor. 80pp. ISBN 0 907758 £2.70. The only book on the natural waters of Derbyshire. Illustrated. Gazetteer of sites.

Joseph Whitworth, Toolmaker Terence Kilburn. 64pp. ISBN 0 907758 22 3 £3.00. The life of the great Victorian engineer and his connection with Darley Dale, Matlock.

Hanged for a Sheep - Crime in Bygone Derbyshire E.G. Power. 80pp. ISBN 0 907758 00 2 £3.00. A factual but entertaining survey of law and order in Derbyshire c.1750-1850.

St. John's Chapel, Belper - The Life of a Church and a Community E.G. Power. 40pp. ISBN 0 907758 11 8 £1.95. The Foresters' Chapel and the people it served from the thirteenth century to the present day.

The Crich Tales - Unexpurgated Echoes from a Derbyshire Village Geoffrey Dawes. 96pp. ISBN 0 907758 06 1. £3.25. Original illustrations by Geoff Taylor. Earthy annecdotes collected in a village pub.

Our Village - Alison Uttley's Cromford Alison Uttley. 72pp. ISBN 0 907758 08 8 £3.00. A selection of her essays, vividly recalling the village scenes of her childhood. The original illustrations by C.F. Tunnicliffe.

Journey from Darkness Gordon Ottewell. 96pp. ISBN 0 907758 02 9 £2.85. Illustrated adventure story for older children about a pit-boy's journey with his pony through Victorian Derbyshire.

ROBERT BAKEWELL - ARTIST BLACKSMITH S. Dunkerley. 112pp. ISBN 0 907758 24 £20.00. Quarto hardback bound in high quality cloth. Thirty-two pages of colour photographs with opposing pages of commentary form the core of this unique life of the great eighteenth century craftsman in wrought iron. Explanatory line drawings. Gazetteer. Edition limited to 750 signed copies.

THE FAMILY WALKS SERIES

Each book has sixteen short, circular walks, specially devised to introduce children to the delights of country walking, and to make the process as trouble-free as possible for parents.

Family Walks in the White Peak Norman Taylor. ISBN 0 907758 09 6 £3.00.

Family Walks in the Dark Peak Norman Taylor. ISBN 0 907758 16 9 £3.00

Family Walks in South Yorkshire Norman Taylor. ISBN 0 907758 25 8 £3.00

Other titles cover Cotswolds; Wiltshire; Hereford and Worcester; Bristol, Bath and the Mendips; Mid Wales; the Wye Valley (Hereford/Monmouth). Cheshire, Shropshire and others in preparation.

Scarthin Books of Cromford are the leading Peak District specialists in secondhand and antiquarian books, and are particularly interested in the field of local history and industrial archaeology.

Contact: Dr. D.J. Mitchell.